An Island Garden

Celia Thaxter in her garden.

An Island Garden

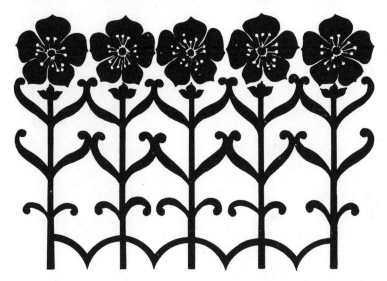

by Celia Thaxter
Illustrated by Childe Hassam
with a new introduction
by John M. Kingsbury

BULLBRIER PRESS
Ithaca, N.Y.
1985

First published in 1894, this edition of *An Island Garden* is often called the Childe Hassam edition because of the color illustrations by Hassam. In this reprint edition, all of these illustrations are reproduced in black and white in the same positions as in the original volume. All of them also are faithfully rendered in full color in a separate section. John M. Kingsbury, former director of the Shoals Marine Laboratory, has indexed the book and written a new introduction. Additional photographs are from the collections of the University of New Hampshire and Frederick T. McGill, Jr. Special appreciation goes to Miss Rosamond Thaxter for her infectious and unflagging interest in the Shoals Marine Laboratory which in its own way led to the recreation of her grandmother's garden on Appledore, and for her cooperation in presenting this reprint edition of Celia Thaxter's last publication. Peter Randall had a considerable mostly invisible but no less important hand in this, too.

More information about the newly recreated garden and the educational program of the Shoals Marine Laboratory may be obtained from the Shoals Marine Laboratory, Cornell University, Ithaca, NY 14853.

This edition commemorates the 150th anniversary of Celia Thaxter's birth.

Bullbrier Press
Ten Snyder Heights
Ithaca, NY 14850

Library of Congress Cataloging-in-Publication Data

Thaxter, Celia, 1835–1894.
    An island garden.

    Reprint. Originally publsihed: Bowie, MD. :
Heritage Books, 1978.
    Bibliography: p.
    Includes index.
    1. Celia Thaxter's Garden (Appledore Island, Me.)
2. Thaxter, Celia, 1835–1894. 3. Gardens—Maine—
Appledore Island. 4. Appledore Island (Me.)—Description
and travel. I. Title.
SB466.U7C458   1985   635'.09741'95   85-13452
ISBN 0-9612610-0-5 (alk. paper)

Introduction to the 1985 Edition

Celia Laighton Thaxter (1835-1894) spent her early childhood on White Island, a minute spot of rock well offshore in the Southern Gulf of Maine. She grew up totally isolated from the mainland, but in the midst of a warm, educated, and enveloping family. Her father, well-born and a rising influence in the business and political life of Portsmouth, New Hampshire, had accepted the position of lighthouse keeper at the Isles of Shoals when Celia was just four years old. Thomas Laighton removed to this unlikely spot because he had hoped that he could reverse the economic decline of the Shoals, earlier a major fishing and trading port, at profit to himself. Thus it came about in 1839 that Celia, her mother, and her baby brother (another was born soon), crossed ten miles of open water separating the Shoals from Portsmouth, climbed out of a small dory onto the granite rock of a tiny treeless island, and occupied a lighthouse and keeper's cottage built twenty years earlier.

White and Seavey Islands, connected by a coarse gravel bar at low tide, together present less than ten acres of surface above high tide line. Most of White is a high promontory of bare granite facing into the Atlantic, meeting the storm waves of the open ocean like a giant fist. Only on the lower western edge of White and on Seavey, lying in its lee, is there soil to support growing plants, and only rugged plants can survive the winds and salt spray whipping across the 160 yards separating shore from shore. As Celia writes in this book, to "a lonely child, living on the lighthouse island ten miles away from the mainland, every blade of grass that sprang out of the ground, every humblest weed, was precious in my sight".

When Celia was twelve years old her father built the Appledore House and ferried his young family the short distance from White Island to their new home. With about 95 acres of surface and three miles of shoreline, Appledore is the largest of the Isles of Shoals. Its topography is rugged, with bluffs, cobble beaches, tidal pools, sharp-edged valleys, and wet areas. Deep deposits of gravel till are found in some places, thin organic soils (which will burn if ignited) in others, and bare granite along exposed shores and elevations. Although Captain John Smith described Appledore as treeless even in 1614, Celia found waiting on this island a whole new world of plants and animals. Windpruned shrubs and bushes and a few stunted trees grew in the sheltered valleys. The remains of home gardens marked by stone walls and a few remnants of cultivated species were still identifiable behind the cottage foundations of the early village on the southern half of the island. Scores of unfamiliar wildflowers populated the valleys, glades, and wet spots. At a most impressionable age, with minds devoid of mainland experience, and with eyes sharpened to nature's ways by the rigors of White Island, Celia and her brothers set out to explore, discover, and learn.

One could say Celia's childhood was deprived and constricted by island circumstances. The opposite was true. The proof is in her writings.

Surrounded by books and deeply influenced by the occasional distinguished visitor to White and then Appledore, Celia began to order her thoughts and the natural images of her childhood and fashion them into words. After marriage to Levi Lincoln Thaxter, her tutor on Appledore, Celia moved with him to the mainland each winter. She expressed some of the intense homesickness she felt for the now distant islands in a poem which passed without her knowledge to the editor of the Atlantic Monthly, who immediately published it under the title "Landlocked". This sudden exposure in the pinnacle of contemporary literary publications evoked important notice. More pieces of poetry and prose were submitted and published there and elsewhere. Soon Celia Thaxter had achieved a measure of fame among those of conservative literary tradition, and she attracted the literary and artistic great of New England to the Appledore House.

The Appledore House was one of the first, and soon became one of the foremost of resort hotels in America. Its register received the signatures of such as Thomas Bailey Aldrich,

Henry Ward Beecher, Ole Bull, Richard Henry Dana, Childe Hassam, Nathaniel Hawthorne, William Dean Howells, William Morris Hunt, Samuel Longfellow, James Russell Lowell, Harriet Beecher Stowe, and John Greenleaf Whittier.

Childe Hassam (1859-1935), the illustrator of *An Island Garden*, was among the first Americans to bring to these shores the impressionist style of painting which he learned in Paris in the late 1880's. As he employed it, this style emphasized the use of color to create a quality of shimmering light and airiness in depicting chosen subjects. The illustrations in this book are good examples of Hassam's style. The originals are in the permanent collection of the Smithsonian Institution. Hassam visited Appledore repeatedly and Shoals subjects figure in many of his major works.

When her parents died, Celia Thaxter moved into their "cottage", a three-story frame building near the hotel. Her parlor contained a grand piano and was filled in the Victorian fashion with paintings, photographs, vases, and flowers. An invitation to attend within these walls an evening of music or readings was an event of signal honor for hotel guests.

The visitor to Celia Thaxter's parlor first passed through the fenced garden in front of the cottage. Just when this garden was first established is not known, but during her lifetime Celia developed and refined it, trying new varieties and propagating old favorites. Eventually the garden in front of the cottage became nearly as famous as the parlor within.

An Island Garden describes Celia's garden as it was in 1893, the last year of her life. In it is distilled a lifetime of acute nature observation at the Shoals, unceasing experimentation, and nurturing of growing things. Even after Celia's death, her garden continued to attract throngs of visitors. In the words of Barbara Laighton Durant, "After Aunt Celia died, when I was only two years old, we moved over to the Thaxter cottage from the Laighton Cottage and my mother kept up the parlor in as nearly the same arrangement as she could manage, and she took charge of the garden. I remember best the wonderful sweet peas against the fence which had a gate down to the well and to the walk which went up to the

hotel from the wharf. I remember what seemed like hordes of
visitors—"trippers"—coming on the morning boat which got
in about 12 and left at 3 or 3:30. They all made straight for
Aunt Celia's parlor and swirled about it in a jam, looking at
the pictures on the wall and the garden and the corner where
she painted which was crowded with slender vases filled with
those delicate and lovely poppies. I remember the migonette
which smelled so sweet and the poppies and of course many
others—nasturtiums, lilies, etc. etc. One time my mother let a
kind and devoted boarder weed one of the beds—as I remember, the beds were boxed in with wooden partitions—but this
helpful lady left the weeds and pulled up the plants—alas!"

An Island Garden is practical to a surprising degree in a
work of literary quality. Celia Thaxter tells us exactly how
the garden was planted, what plant varieties she used, just
where she put them in the garden, how she weeded, pruned,
and watered. She describes her battles with insects and the
enemy slug, competition with birds, the finer points of fer-
tilization. In brief, she provided enough detail to reestablish
the garden exactly as it was in 1893. The Shoals Marine Laboratory (present inhabitant of Appledore Island), the Rye
Beach, Little Boar's Head Garden Club, Cornell Plantations,
several students and special friends joined forces in 1977 to
accomplish just that.

The original garden occupied a terrace immediately in
front of Celia's piazza. Placing it back on the exact same spot
was easy, for Celia gives dimensions, and the foundations of
her cottage (which burned when the hotel burned in 1914) are
readily apparent. Extant photographs show what the fence
and gates were like.

But there were problems. The garden terrace had grown up
to a mature stand of wild cherry, sumac, and witch grass (or
quitch grass as Celia calls it). Celia had the garden spaded
each year. In 1976 the Shoals Lab backhoe grubbed down the
brush, pulled up the largest roots, and cleared the area. During the years of the second world war, Appledore Island had
been occupied by the military. The Army built a barracks
near Celia's cottage foundations, in the process removing a

corner of the terrace. In 1977 that terrace had to be rebuilt, and suitable soil is scarce on Appledore. Finally, the rebuilt terrace and cleared area was subjected to intense attack by a rototiller to chop up the grass roots and those remaining from the woody brush.

In the reconstruction of Celia Thaxter's garden, comparing how things were done then with now was particularly interesting. Backhoe and rototiller against spade and wheelbarrow is one of the more dramatic comparisons. Such comparisons show that major changes have occurred during the 80-odd years separating Celia's original garden from the reconstructed one. This particular example is mechanical. Other equally dramatic differences relate to changes in island biology.

Celia had a great deal of trouble with sparrows and other seed-eating birds which descended on the garden in hordes. She had to cover the newly planted beds with boards or fish nets to preserve any seeds for sprouting. That problem did not arise in 1977. The tremendous numbers of gulls now on Appledore undoubtedly discourage large flocks of seed-eating birds. Gulls were comparatively rare in 1893. Today's gulls are responsible, too, for another less obvious difference. In dry weather, Celia watered her garden daily with a hose. Where did she get the water? Fresh water is now a scarce and precious commodity on Appledore. It cannot easily be spared for watering gardens. Granted the human population of Appledore is conditioned to use greater quantities of fresh water in daily life than was the custom in the 1890's, and granted also that the Appledore House had supplemental means of storage lacking now, nevertheless the supply of fresh water was greater on Appledore then than now. Then, rainwater was collected on the roofs and used in the domestic water system (collecting gutters and downspouts are unequivocal in pictures of the hotel). The large numbers of gulls roosting on the roofs of all island buildings today render water collected thus unsuitable for the island system.

Celia was troubled primarily by slugs. She tells how they were inadvertently introduced to the island and devotes many paragraphs to the subsequent relentless battle she waged to keep their depredations within bounds. No slugs at all were discovered in the reconstructed garden in 1977. Maybe they have again become absent on Appledore.

Another major pest has been introduced, however, in the years betwen 1890 and 1977—the muskrat. Shoals Lab biologists estimate there are around 300 of these animals now on the island and thriving. Their island diet is somewhat different from what they eat on the mainland. On Appledore they eat voraciously of the herbaceous vegetation, and no garden can be successful without protection from them. The new garden has a perimeter of chicken wire attached to the board fence, dug a foot into the soil.

Celia started many of her plants for the Appledore garden in her Portsmouth winter home. Some don't transplant easily if the roots are disturbed. These she planted in egg shells, breaking the shell from the ball of soil as she placed the seedling in its final location in the garden. Today the seedlings are started in the greenhouses of The Thompson School, University of New Hampshire, and are transported to Appledore in the usual commercial flat, a technique less romantic perhaps than egg shells, but requiring less careful handling on the boat trip from the mainland.

A stark comparison exists between pest control then and now. Celia was bothered with a large number of pests—insects, fungi, slugs. She catalogs early in *An Island Garden* her extensive armamentarium of pesticides and the care and discrimination necessary in their use. Under the best of circumstances many of these materials were only marginally effective. The garden of 1977 had few pest problems and modern pesticides (used with even more care and discrimination) readily take care of this kind of problem when it does arise.

Horses, sheep, pigs, and one or two cows lived on Appledore during the years of the hotel, performing the functions by which these animals have served man since prehistory. They also furnished manure for Celia's garden. She had only to ask. She had lime, too, brought out from the mainland. The 1977 garden had neither lime nor fertilizer, organic or otherwise. It grew luxuriantly without these aids. However, as the sods decomposed, the high natural fertility of the soil decreased. Unfortunately the island's livestock population is now reduced to only two pigs. Their droppings and those of the ubiquitous gulls are too dispersed for practical use. Imported humus (peat moss mostly) and commercial fertilizer applied with a very light touch are now used to recreate the lushness of vegetation shown in Hassam's paintings.

Why did Celia's garden have such a heavy board fence? Rebuilding the garden has suggested an original purpose for this fence that we might othewise not have guessed. Not for keeping people out, nor keeping livestock out either, as might at first be thought, the fence manifested its true importance to the garden of 1977 as the plants grew within. It keeps them from being flattened by the nearly constant and often strong winds experienced on a remote offshore island.

In Celia's day the fence served also to keep dogs out. In her fight with slugs, Celia finally enlisted the aid of imported toads. But she mentions that both toads and frogs had a difficult existence on Appledore because of the dogs. Today dogs (and cats) are rigidly excluded from even setting foot on the island. The State of Maine has officially declared the heron rookery on Appledore to be a critical natural area. The exclusion of pets is for the purpose of protecting the populations of unusual nesting marine and migratory birds.

The seasons have not changed on Appledore. May first is still the earliest dependable frost-free date. But garden plants themselves have changed tremendously since the 1890's. This is perhaps the greatest and most interesting change between then and now. Few of the varieties that were new or common in Celia's day are common today. Many of those she names are no longer available through commercial channels. Even with the help of botanical gardens and other repositories of old varieties it is a slow matter to locate and procure authentic genetic replacement for all of Celia's materials. But that is the aim. In 1977, in its first season, the reconstructed garden had about one-quarter of the "right" things. It now has many more. But finding the last of more than 50 kinds listed in *An Island Garden* may be a long task. As a last resort, it may even be necessary to breed back toward certain plant materials if they can no longer be found. This is not an impossible task, given sufficient interest and support.

The reconstruction of Celia Thaxter's garden is backed by the support of horticultural experts at Cornell University and the University of New Hampshire, the parent institutions of the Shoals Marine Laboratory. Its yearly planting and weekly management are undertaken by a group of dedicated seacoast garden club members under the enthusiastic leadership of Virginia Chisholm. Few historic gardens are as well described as this, and few reconstructions have yet been attempted from this particular period of American history. No other has the special charm of being located on a small isolated island. The holder of this volume has the description by Celia Thaxter and the depiction by Childe Hassam in his hand. The summer visitor to Appledore Island can once again walk among the beds of flowers and experience the botanical tapestry that inspired the original creators of this volume.

John M. Kingsbury

The interested reader can flesh out this bareboned outline of the life and interests of Celia Laighton Thaxter in her own writings (see especially Poems by Celia Thaxter *and* Among the Isles of Shoals), Letters to Celia *by Frederick T. McGill, Jr., and* Sandpiper, *the* Life and Letters of Celia Thaxter, *a biography by her granddaughter Rosamond Thaxter. Other interesting publications are:* Celia Thaxter: Seeker of the Unattainable *by Perry D. Westbrook in* Colby Literary Quarterly, December 1964; A Stern and Lovely Scene: A Visual History of the Isles of Shoals, *University Art Galleries, University of New Hampshire, 1978;* Celia Thaxter and her Island Garden *by Katharine L. Jacobs in* Landscape, 24, 1980; *and* Poet's Garden, Painter's Eye *by Deborah Nevins in* House and Garden, August, 1984. Celia Thaxter is buried with her mother, father, and brothers in the Laighton Cemetery on Appledore Island. Appledore's wild plants of today are described in* The Vascular Flora of Appledore Island *by Gary Boden, published by the Shoals Marine Laboratory, 1977; and in* Remarks on the more Conspicuous Vascular Plants, Appledore Island, Isles of Shoals, Maine *by Carl J. George, published by Union College, 1979.*

A corner of the reconstructed garden.

In the Garden

AN ISLAND GARDEN

BY CELIA THAXTER
WITH PICTURES AND
ILLUMINATIONS BY
CHILDE HASSAM

BOSTON AND NEW YORK
HOUGHTON MIFFLIN & CO.
The Riverside Press, Cambridge
MDCCCXCV

The Riverside Press, Cambridge, Mass., U. S. A.
Electrotyped and Printed by H. O. Houghton & Company.

TO

MRS. MARY HEMENWAY

"WHOSE LARGENESS OF HEART IS EVEN AS THE

SAND ON THE SEASHORE"

THIS VOLUME

IS AFFECTIONATELY INSCRIBED

T the Isles of Shoals, among the ledges of the largest island, Appledore, lies the small garden which in the following pages I have endeavored to describe. Ever since I could remember anything, flowers have been like dear friends to me, comforters, inspirers, powers to uplift and to cheer. A lonely child, living on the lighthouse island ten miles away from the mainland, every blade of grass that sprang out of the ground, every humblest weed, was precious in my sight, and I began a little garden when not more than five years old. From this, year after year, the larger one, which has given so much pleasure to so many people, has grown. The first small bed at the lighthouse island contained only Marigolds, pot Marigolds, fire-colored blossoms which were the joy of my heart and the delight of my eyes. This scrap of garden, literally not more than a

yard square, with its barbaric splendors of color,
I worshiped like any Parsee. When I planted
the dry, brown seeds I noticed how they were
shaped, like crescents, with a fine line of orna-
mental dots, a " beading " along the whole length
of the centre, — from this crescent sprang the
Marigold plant, each of whose flowers was like

> " a mimic sun,
> With ray-like florets round a disk-like face."

In my childish mind I pondered much on this
fact of the crescent growing into the full-rayed
orb. Many thoughts had I of all the flowers I
knew; very dear were they, so that after I had
gathered them I felt sorry, and I had a safe place
between the rocks to which I carried them when
they were withered, and hid them away from all
eyes, they were so precious even then.

The dear flowers! Summer after summer they
return to me, always young and fresh and beautiful; but so many of the friends who have watched
them and loved them with me are gone, and they
return no more. I think of the lament of Mos-
chus for Bion : —

" Ah me, when the Mallows wither in the garden, and the green Parsley, and the curled tendrils of the Anise, on a later day they spring, in
another year; but we men, we, the great and
mighty, or wise, when once we have died, in hollow earth we sleep, gone down into silence."

Into silence! How deep, how unbroken is that
silence! But because of tender memories of loving eyes that see them no more, my flowers are
yet more beloved and tenderly cherished.

Year after year the island garden has grown
in beauty and charm, so that in response to the
many entreaties of strangers as well as friends
who have said to me, summer after summer,
" Tell us how you do it! Write a book about it
and tell us how it is done, that we may go also
and do likewise," I have written this book at last.
Truly it contains the fruit of much sweet and
bitter experience. Of what I speak I know, and
of what I know I have freely given. I trust it
may help the patient gardener to a reasonable
measure of success, and to that end I have spared
no smallest detail that seemed to me necessary, no
suggestion that might prove helpful.

DUST.

Here is a problem, a wonder for all to see.
    Look at this marvelous thing I hold in my hand!
This is a magic surprising, a mystery
    Strange as a miracle, harder to understand.

What is it ? Only a handful of earth : to your touch
    A dry rough powder you trample beneath your feet,
Dark and lifeless ; but think for a moment, how much
    It hides and holds that is beautiful, bitter, or sweet.

Think of the glory of color! The red of the rose,
  Green of the myriad leaves and the fields of grass,
Yellow as bright as the sun where the daffodil blows,
  Purple where violets nod as the breezes pass.

Think of the manifold form, of the oak and the vine,
  Nut, and fruit, and cluster, and ears of corn;
Of the anchored water-lily, a thing divine,
  Unfolding its dazzling snow to the kiss of morn.

Think of the delicate perfumes borne on the gale,
  Of the golden willow catkin's odor of spring,
Of the breath of the rich narcissus waxen-pale,
  Of the sweet pea's flight of flowers, of the nettle's sting.

Strange that this lifeless thing gives vine, flower, tree,
  Color and shape and character, fragrance too;
That the timber that builds the house, the ship for the sea,
  Out of this powder its strength and its toughness drew!

That the cocoa among the palms should suck its milk
  From this dry dust, while dates from the self-same soil
Summon their sweet rich fruit: that our shining silk
  The mulberry leaves should yield to the worm's slow toil.

How should the poppy steal sleep from the very source
  That grants to the grapevine juice that can madden or
    cheer?
How does the weed find food for its fabric coarse
  Where the lilies proud their blossoms pure uprear?

Who shall compass or fathom God's thought profound?
  We can but praise, for we may not understand;
But there's no more beautiful riddle the whole world round
  Than is hid in this heap of dust I hold in my hand.

THE LIST OF PICTURES FOR AN
ARDEN

AN ISLAND GARDEN
BY CELIA THAXTER

WITH PAINTINGS BY
CHILDE HASSAM

O F all the wonderful things in the wonderful universe of God, nothing seems to me more surprising than the planting of a seed in the blank earth and the result thereof. Take a Poppy seed, for instance: it lies in your palm, the merest atom of matter, hardly visible, a speck, a pin's point in bulk, but within it is imprisoned a spirit of beauty ineffable, which will break its bonds and emerge from the dark ground and blossom in a splendor so dazzling as to baffle all powers of description.

The Genie in the Arabian tale is not half so astonishing. In this tiny casket lie folded roots, stalks, leaves, buds, flowers, seed-vessels, — surpassing color and beautiful form, all that goes to make up a plant which is as gigantic in proportion to the bounds that confine it as the Oak is to the acorn. You may watch this marvel from beginning to end in a few weeks' time, and if you realize how great a marvel it is, you can but be

3

lost in " wonder, love, and praise." All seeds are most interesting, whether winged like the Dandelion and Thistle, to fly on every breeze afar; or barbed to catch in the wool of cattle or the garments of men, to be borne away and spread in all directions over the land; or feathered like the little polished silvery shuttlecocks of the Cornflower, to whirl in the wind abroad and settle presently, point downward, into the hospitable ground; or oared like the Maple, to row out upon the viewless tides of the air. But if I were to pause on the threshold of the year to consider the miracles of seeds alone, I should never, I fear, reach my garden plot at all!

He who is born with a silver spoon in his mouth is generally considered a fortunate person, but his good fortune is small compared to that of the happy mortal who enters this world with a passion for flowers in his soul. I use the word advisedly, though it seems a weighty one for the subject, for I do not mean a light or shallow affection, or even an æsthetic admiration; no butterfly interest, but a real love which is worthy of the name, which is capable of the dignity of sacrifice, great enough to bear discomfort of body and disappointment of spirit, strong enough to fight a thousand enemies for the thing beloved, with power, with judgment, with endless patience, and to give with everything else a subtler stimulus which is more delicate and perhaps more necessary than all the rest.

Often I hear people say, " How do you make your plants flourish like this?" as they admire the little flower patch I cultivate in summer, or the window gardens that bloom for me in the winter; " I can never make my plants blossom like this! What is your secret?" And I answer with one word, " Love." For that includes all, — the patience that endures continual trial, the constancy that makes perseverance possible, the power of foregoing ease of mind and body to minister to the necessities of the thing beloved, and the subtle bond of sympathy which is as important, if not more so, than all the rest. For though I cannot go so far as a witty friend of mine, who says that when he goes out to sit in the shade on his piazza, his Wistaria vine leans toward him and lays her head on his shoulder, I am fully and intensely aware that plants are conscious of love and respond to it as they do to nothing else. You may give them all they need of food and drink and make the conditions of their existence as favorable as possible, and they may grow and bloom, but there is a certain ineffable something that will be missing if you do not love them, a delicate glory too spiritual to be caught and put into words. The Norwegians have a pretty and significant word, " Opelske," which they use in speaking of the care of flowers. It means literally " loving up," or cherishing them into health and vigor.

Like the musician, the painter, the poet, and the rest, the true lover of flowers is born, not made. And he is born to happiness in this vale of tears, to a certain amount of the purest joy that earth can give her children, joy that is tranquil, innocent, uplifting, unfailing. Given a little patch of ground, with time to take care of it, with tools to work it and seeds to plant in it, he has all he needs, and Nature with her dews and suns and showers and sweet airs gives him her aid. But he soon learns that it is not only liberty of which eternal vigilance is the price; the saying applies quite as truly to the culture of flowers, for the name of their enemies is legion, and they must be fought early and late, day and night, without cessation. The cutworm, the wire-worm, the pansy-worm, the thrip, the rose-beetle, the aphis, the mildew, and many more, but worst of all the loathsome slug, a slimy, shapeless creature that devours every fair and exquisite thing in the garden, — the flower lover must seek all these with unflagging energy, and if possible exterminate the whole. So only may he and his precious flowers purchase peace. Manifold are the means of destruction to be employed, for almost every pest requires a different poison. On a closet shelf which I keep especially for them are rows of tin pepper-boxes, each containing a deadly powder, all carefully labeled. For the thrip that eats out the leaves of the Rosebush till they are nothing but fibrous skeletons of woody lace, there is hellebore, to be shaken on the under side of all the leaves, — mark you, the *under* side, and think of the difficulties involved in the process of so treating hundreds of leaves! For the blue or gray mildew and the orange mildew another box holds powdered sulphur, — this is more easily applied, shaken over the tops of the bushes, but all the

leaves must be reached, none neglected at your
peril! Still another box contains yellow snuff
for the green aphis, but he is almost impossible
to manage, — let once his legions get a foothold,
good-by to any hope for you! Lime, salt, paris
green, cayenne pepper, kerosene emulsion, whale-
oil soap, the list of weapons is long indeed, with
which one must fight the garden's foes! And it
must be done with such judgment, persistence,
patience, accuracy, and watchful care! It seems
to me the worst of all the plagues is the slug,
the snail without a shell. He is beyond description repulsive, a mass of sooty, shapeless slime,
and he devours everything. He seems to thrive
on all the poisons known; salt and lime are the
only things that have power upon him, at least
the only things I have been able to find so far.
But salt and lime must be used very carefully, or
they destroy the plant as effectually as the slug
would do. Every night, while the season is yet
young, and the precious growths just beginning
to make their way upward, feeling their strength,
I go at sunset and heap along the edge of the
flower beds air-slaked lime, or round certain most
valuable plants a ring of the same, — the slug
cannot cross this while it is fresh, but should it
be left a day or two it loses its strength, it has no
more power to burn, and the enemy may slide
over it unharmed, leaving his track of slime. On
many a solemn midnight have I stolen from my
bed to visit my cherished treasures by the pale
glimpses of the moon, that I might be quite sure
the protecting rings were still strong enough to

save them, for the slug eats by night, he is invisible by day unless it rains or the sky be overcast. He hides under every damp board or in any nook of shade, because the sun is death to him. I use salt for his destruction in the same way as the lime, but it is so dangerous for the plants, I am always afraid of it. Neither of these things must be left about them when they are watered lest the lime or salt sink into the earth in such quantities as to injure the tender roots. I have little cages of fine wire netting which I adjust over some plants, carefully heaping the earth about them to leave no loophole through which the enemy may crawl, and round some of the beds, which are inclosed in strips of wood, boxed, to hold the earth in place, long shallow troughs of wood are nailed and filled with salt to keep off the pests. Nothing that human ingenuity can suggest do I leave untried to save my beloved flowers! Every evening at sunset I pile lime and salt about my pets, and every morning remove it before I sprinkle them at sunrise. The salt dissolves of itself in the humid sea air and in the dew, so around those for whose safety I am most solicitous I lay rings of pasteboard on which to heap it, to be certain of doing the plants no harm. Judge, reader, whether all this requires strength, patience, perseverance, hope! It is hard work beyond a doubt, but I do not grudge it, for great is my reward. Before I knew what to do to save my garden from the slugs, I have stood at evening rejoicing over rows of fresh emerald leaves just springing in rich lines along the beds, and woke in the morning to find the whole space stripped of any sign of green, as blank as a board over which a carpenter's plane has passed.

In the thickest of my fight with the slugs some one said to me, " Everything living has its enemy; the enemy of the slug is the toad. Why don't you import toads? "

I snatched at the hope held out to me, and immediately wrote to a friend on the continent, " In the name of the Prophet, Toads! " At once a force of only too willing boys was set about the work of catching every toad within reach, and one day in June a boat brought a box to me from the far-off express office. A piece of wire netting was nailed across the top, and upon the earth with which it was half filled, reposing among some dry and dusty green leaves, sat three dry and dusty toads, wearily gazing at nothing. Is this all, I thought, only three! Hardly worth sending so far. Poor creatures, they looked so arid and wilted, I took up the hose and turned upon them a gentle shower of fresh cool water, flooding the box. I was not prepared for the result! The dry, baked earth heaved tumultuously; up came dusky heads and shoulders and bright eyes by the dozen. A sudden concert of liquid sweet notes was poured out on the air from the whole rejoicing company. It was really beautiful to hear that musical ripple of delight. I surveyed them with eager interest as they sat singing and blinking together. "You are not handsome," I said, as I took a hammer and wrenched off the wire cover that shut them in, "but you will be lovely in my sight if you will help me to destroy mine enemy;" and with that I turned the box on its side and out they skipped into a perfect paradise of food and shade. All summer I came upon them in different parts of the garden, waxing fatter and fatter till they were as round as apples. In the autumn baby toads no larger than my thumb nail were found hopping merrily over the whole island. There were sixty in that first importation; next summer I received ninety more. But alas! small dogs discover them in the grass and delight to tear and worry them to death, and the rats prey upon them so that many perish in that way; yet I hope to keep enough to preserve my garden in spite of fate.

In France the sale of toads for the protection of gardens is universal, and I find under the head of "A Garden Friend," in a current newspaper, the following item : —

"One is amused, in walking through the great Covent Garden Market, London, to find toads among the commodities offered for sale. In such favor do these familiar reptiles stand with English market gardeners that they readily command a shilling apiece. . . . The toad has indeed no superior as a destroyer of noxious insects, and as he possesses no bad habits and is entirely inoffensive himself, every owner of a garden should treat him with the utmost hospitality. It is quite worth the while not only to offer any simple inducements which suggest themselves for rendering the premises attractive to him, but should he show a tendency to wander away from them, to

From the Doorway

*Celia's cottage and fenced garden. Upper photo Isles of Shoals
Collection, UNH Media Services. Courtesy Star Island Corporation.*

go so far as to exercise a gentle force in bringing him back to the regions where his services may be of the greatest utility."

One of the most universal pests is the cutworm, a fat, naked worm of varying lengths. I have seen them two inches and a half long and as large round as my little finger. This unpleasant creature lives in the ground about the roots of plants. I have known one to go through a whole row of Sweet Peas and cut them off smoothly above the roots just as a sickle would do; there lay the dead stalks in melancholy line. It makes no difference what the plant may be, they will level all without distinction. The only remedy for this plague is to scratch all about in the earth round the roots of the plants where their ravages begin, dig the worms out, and kill them. I have found sometimes whole nests of them with twenty young ones at once. Lime dug into the soil is recommended to destroy them, but there is no remedy so sure as seeking a personal interview and slaying them on the spot. They are not by any means always to be discovered, but the gardener must again exercise that endless patience upon which the success of the garden depends, and be never weary of seeking them till they are found.

Another enemy to my flowers, and a truly formidable one, is my little friend the song-sparrow. Literally he gives the plot of ground no peace if I venture to put seeds into it. He obliges me to start almost all my seeds in boxes, to be transplanted into the beds when the plants are sufficiently tough to have lost their delicacy for his palate and are no longer adapted to his ideal of a salad. All the Sweet Peas, many hundreds of the delicate plants, are every one grown in this way. When they are a foot high with roots a foot long they are all transplanted separately. Even then the little robber attacks them, and, though he cannot uproot, he will "yank" and twist the stems till he has murdered them in the vain hope of pulling up the remnant of a pea which he judges to be somewhere beneath the surface. Then must sticks and supports be draped with yards of old fishing nets to protect the unfortunates, and over the Mignonette, and even the Poppy beds and others, I must lay a cover of closely woven wire to keep out the marauder. But I love him still, though sadly he torments me. I have adored his fresh music ever since I was a child, and I only laugh as he sits on the fence watching me with his bright black eyes; there is something quaintly comical and delightful about him, and he sings like a friendly angel. From him I can protect myself, but I cannot save my garden so easily from the hideous slug, for which I have no sentiment save only a fury of extermination.

If possible, it is much the best way to begin in the autumn to work for the garden of the next spring, and the first necessity is the preparation of the soil. If the gardener is as fortunate as I am at the Isles of Shoals, there will be no trouble in doing this, for there the barn manure is heaped in certain waste places, out of the way, and left till every change of wind and weather, of temperature and climate, have so wrought upon it that it becomes a fine, odorless, velvet-brown earth, rich in all needful sustenance for almost all plants, — " well-rotted manure," the " Old Farmer's Almanac " calls it. But if there is no mine of wealth such as this from which to draw, there are many fertilizers, sold by all seed and plant merchants, which will answer the purpose very well. I have, however, never found anything to equal barn manure as food for flowers, and if not possible to obtain this in a state fit for immediate use, it is best to have several cart-loads taken from the barn in autumn and piled in a heap near the garden plot, there to remain all winter, till rains and snows and cold and heat, all the powers of the elements, have worked their will upon it, and rendered it fit for use in the coming spring. Many people make a compost heap, — it is an excellent thing to do, — piling turf and dead leaves and refuse together, and leaving it to slow decay till it becomes a fine, rich, mellow earth. In my case the barn manure has been more easily obtained, and so I have used it always and with complete success, but I have a compost heap also, to use for plants which do not like barn manure.

As late as possible, before the ground freezes, I dig up the single Dahlia tubers (there are no double ones in my garden), and put them in boxes filled with clean, dry sand, to keep in a frost-free cellar till spring. I find Gladiolus bulbs, Tulips, Lilies, and so forth, will keep perfectly well in the ground through the winter at the Shoals.

Over the Foxgloves, Iceland Poppies, Wallflowers,
Mullein Pinks, Picotees, and other perennials, I
scatter the fine barn manure lightly, over the
Hollyhocks more heavily, and about the Rosebushes I heap it up high, quite two thirds of their
whole height, — you cannot give them too much,
only be careful that enough of their length, that
is to say, one third of the highest sprays, are left
out in the air, that they may breathe. In the
spring this manure must all be carefully dug into
the ground round their roots. About Honeysuckles, Clematis, Grapevine, and so forth, I pile it
plentifully, mixed with wood ashes, which is especially good for Grapevine and Rosebushes. But
the white Lilies, and indeed Lilies generally, do
not like to come in contact with the barn manure,
so they are protected by leaves and boughs, and
the earth near them enriched in the spring, carefully avoiding the contact which they dislike.
When putting the garden in order in the autumn,
all the dry Sweet Pea vines, and dead stalks of all
kinds, which are pulled up to clear the ground, I
heap for shelter over the perennials, being careful
to lay small bayberry branches over first, so that
I may in no way interfere with a free circulation
of air about them. In open spaces where no
perennials are growing I scatter the manure
thickly, that the ground may be slowly and surely
enriched all through the winter and be ready to
furnish bountiful nourishment for every green
growing thing through the summer. When the
little plot is spaded in April, all this is dug in and
mixed thoroughly with the soil.

When the snow is still blowing against the
window-pane in January and February, and the
wild winds are howling without, what pleasure it
is to plan for summer that is to be! Small shallow wooden boxes are ready, filled with mellow
earth (of which I am always careful to lay in a
supply before the ground freezes in the autumn),
sifted and made damp; into it the precious seeds
are dropped with a loving hand. The Pansy
seeds lie like grains of gold on the dark soil. I
think as I look at them of the splendors of impe-
rial purples folded within them, of their gold and
blue and bronze, of all the myriad combinations
of superb color in their rich velvets. Each one of
these small golden grains means such a wealth
of beauty and delight! Then the thin flake-like
brown seeds of the annual Stocks or Gillyflowers;
one little square of paper holds the white Princess
Alice variety, so many thick double spikes of
fragrant snow lie hidden in each thin dry flake!
Another paper holds the pale rose-color, another
the delicate lilacs, or deep purples, or shrimp
pinks, or vivid crimsons, — all are dropped on the
earth, lightly covered, gently pressed down; then
sprinkled and set in a warm place, they are left to
germinate. Next I come to the single Dahlia
seeds, rough, dry, misshapen husks, that, being
planted thus early, will blossom by the last of
June, unfolding their large rich stars in great
abundance till frost. They blossom in every
variety of color except blue; all shades of red
from faint rose to black maroon, and all are gold-
centred. They are every shade of yellow from

sulphur to flame, — king's flowers, I call them,
stately and splendid.

All these and many more are planted. For
those that do not bear transplanting I prepare
other quarters, half filling shallow boxes with
sand, into which I set rows of egg-shells close
together, each shell cut off at one end, with a
hole for drainage at the bottom. These are filled
with earth, and in them the seeds of the lovely
yellow, white, and orange Iceland Poppies are
sowed. By and by, when comes the happy time
for setting them out in the garden beds, the shell
can be broken away from the oval ball of earth that
holds their roots without disturbing them, and
they are transplanted almost without knowing it.
It is curious how differently certain plants feel
about this matter of transplanting. The more
you move a Pansy about the better it seems to
like it, and many annuals grow all the better for
one transplanting; but to a Poppy it means death,
unless it is done in some such careful way as I
have described.

The boxes of seeds are put in a warm, dark
place, for they only require heat and moisture till
they germinate. Then when the first precious
green leaves begin to appear, what a pleasure it
is to wait and tend on the young growths, which
are moved carefully to some cool, sunny chamber
window in a room where no fire is kept, for heat
becomes the worst enemy at this stage, and they
spindle and dwindle if not protected from it.
When they are large enough, having attained to
their second leaves, each must be put into a little

pot or egg-shell by itself (all except the Poppies and their companions, already in egg-shells), so that by the time the weather is warm enough they will be ready to be set out, stout and strong, for early blooming.

This pleasant business goes on during the winter in the picturesque old town of Portsmouth, New Hampshire, whither I repair in the autumn from the Isles of Shoals, remaining through the cold weather and returning to the islands on the first of April. My upper windows all winter are filled with young Wallflowers, Stocks, single Dahlias, Hollyhocks, Poppies, and many other garden plants, which are watched and tended with the most faithful care till the time comes for transporting them over the seas to Appledore. A small steam tug, the Pinafore, carries me and my household belongings over to the islands, and a pretty sight is the little vessel when she starts out from the old brown wharves and steams away down the beautiful Piscataqua River, with her hurricane deck awave with green leaves and flowers, for all the world like a May Day procession. My blossoming house plants go also, and there are Palms and Ferns and many other lovely things that make the small boat gay indeed. All the boxes of sprouted seedlings are carefully packed in wide square baskets to keep them steady, and the stout young plants hold up their strong stems and healthy green leaves, and take the wind and sun bravely as the vessel goes tossing over the salt waves out to sea.

By the first of April it is time to plant Sweet

Peas. From this time till the second week in May, when one may venture to transplant into the garden, the boxes containing the myriads of seedlings must be carefully watched and tended, put out of doors on piazza roofs and balcony through the days and taken in again at night, solicitously protected from too hot suns and too rough winds, too heavy rains or too low a temperature, — they require continual care. But it is joy to give them all they need, and pleasure indeed to watch their vigorous growth. Meanwhile there is much delightful work to be done in making the small garden plot ready. This little island garden of mine is so small that the amount of pure delight it gives in the course of a summer is something hardly to be credited. It lies along the edge of a piazza forty or fifty feet long, sloping to the south, not more than fifteen feet wide, sheltered from the north winds and open to the sun. The whole piazza is thickly draped with vines, Hops, Honeysuckles, blue and white Clematis, Cinnamon Vine, *Mina Lobata*, Wistaria, Nasturtiums, Morning - glories, Japanese Hops, Woodbine, and the beautiful and picturesque Wild Cucumber (*Echinocystus Lobata*), which in July nearly smothers everything else and clothes itself in a veil of filmy white flowers in loose clusters, fragrant, but never too sweet, always refreshing and exquisite. The vines make a grateful green shade, doubly delightful for that there are no trees on my island, and the shade is most welcome in the wide brilliancy of sea and sky.

In the first week of April the ground is spaded

A Shady Seat

View from Celia Thaxter's piazza through the garden.

for me; after that no hands touch it save my own throughout the whole season. Day after day it is so pleasant working in the bright cool spring air, for as yet the New England spring is alert and brisk in temperature and shows very little softening in its moods. But by the seventh day of the month, as I stand pruning the Rosebushes, there is a flutter of glad wings, and lo! the first house martins! Beautiful creatures, with their white breasts and steel - blue wings, wheeling, chattering, and scolding at me, for they think I stand too near their little brown house on the corner of the piazza eaves, and they let me know their opinion by coming as near as they dare and snapping their beaks at me with a low guttural sound of displeasure. But after a few days, when they have found they cannot scare me and that I do not interfere with them, they conclude that I am a harmless kind of creature and endure me with tranquillity. Straightway they take possession of their summer quarters and begin to build their cosy nest within. Oh, then the weeks of joyful work, the love-making, the cooing, chattering, calling, in tones of the purest delight and content, the tilting against the wind on burnished wings, the wheeling, fluttering, coquetting, and caressing, the while they bring feathers and straw and shreds and down for their nest-weaving, — all this goes on till after the eggs are laid, when they settle down into comparative quiet. Then often the father bird sits and meditates happily in the sun upon his tiny brown chimney-top, while the mother bird broods below. Or they

go out and take a dip in the air together, or sit
conversing in pretty cadences a little space, till
mother bird must hie indoors to the eggs she
dare not leave longer lest they grow chill. And
this sweet little drama is repeated all about the
island, on sunny roofs and corners and tall posts,
wherever a bird house has been built for their
convenience. All through April and May I
watch them as I go to and fro about my business,
while they attend to theirs; we do not interfere
with each other; they have made up their minds
to endure me, but I adore them! Flattered indeed am I if, while I am at work upon the flower
beds below, father martin comes and sits close to
me on the fence rail and chatters musically, unmindful of my quiet movements, quite fearless
and at home.

While I am busy with pleasant preparation
and larger hope, I rejoice in the beauty of the
pure white Snowdrops I found blossoming in their
sunny corner when I arrived on the first of April,
fragile winged things with their delicate sea-green
markings and fresh, grass-like leaves. Ever since
the first of March have they been blossoming,
and the Crocus flowers begin, as if blown out of
the earth, like long, lovely bubbles of gold and
purple, or white, pure or streaked with lilac, to
break, under the noon sun, into beautiful petals,
showing the orange anthers like flame within.
And the little Scilla Siberica hangs its enchanting bells out to the breeze, blue, oh, blue as the
deep sea water at its bluest under cloudless skies.
And later, yellow Daffodils and Jonquils, " Tulips

dashed with fiery dew," the exquisite, mystic poet's Narcissus, and one crimson Peony, — my little garden has not room for more than one of these large plants, so early blossoming and at their end so soon.

In the first week of May every year punctually arrive the barn swallows and the sandpipers at the Isles of Shoals. This seems a very commonplace statement of a very simple fact, but would it were possible to convey in words the sense of delight with which they are welcomed on this sea-surrounded rock !

Some morning in the first of May I sit in the sunshine and soft air, transplanting my young Pansies and Gillyflowers into the garden beds,— father and mother martin on the fence watching me and talking to each other in a charming language, the import of which is clear enough, though my senses are not sufficiently delicate to comprehend the words. The song-sparrows pour out their simple, friendly lays from bush and wall and fence and gable peak all about me. Down in a hollow I hear the brimming note of the white-throated sparrow, — brimming is the only word that expresses it,—like "a beaker full of the warm South," — such joy, such overflowing measure of bliss ! There is a challenge from a robin, perhaps, or a bobolink sends down his "brook o' laughter through the air," or high and far a curlew calls ; there is a gentle lapping of waves from the full tide, for the sea is only a stone's-throw from my garden fence. I hear the voices of the children prattling not far away ; there are no other sounds. Suddenly from the shore comes a clear cry thrice repeated, "Sweet, sweet, sweet!" And I call to my neighbor, my brother, working also in his garden plot, "The sandpiper! Do you hear him?" and the glad news goes from mouth to mouth, "The sandpiper has come!" Oh, the lovely note again and again repeated, "Sweet, sweet, sweet!" echoing softly in the stillness of the tide-brimmed coves, where the quiet water seems to hush itself to listen. Never so tender a cry is uttered by any bird I know; it is the most exquisitely beautiful, caressing tone, heard in the dewy silence of morning and evening. He has many and varied notes and calls, some collo-quial, some business-like, some meditative, and his cry of fear breaks my heart to hear when any evil threatens his beloved nest; but this ten-der call, "Sweet, sweet," is the most enchanting sound, happy with a fullness of joy that never fails to bring a thrill to the heart that listens. It is like the voice of Love itself.

Then out of the high heaven above, at once one hears the happy chorus of the barn swallows; they come rejoicing, their swift wings cleave the blue, they fill the air with woven melody of grace and music. Till late August they remain. Like the martins', their note is pure joy; there is no coloring of sadness in any sound they make. The sandpiper's note is pensive with all its sweet-ness; there is a quality of thoughtfulness, as it were, in the voice of the song-sparrow; the robin has many sad cadences; in the fairy bugling of the oriole there is a triumphant richness, but not such pure delight; the blackbird's call is keen and sweet, but not so glad; and the bobolink, when he shakes those brilliant jewels of sound from his bright throat, is always the prince of jokers, full of fun, but not so happy as comical. The swallows' twittering seems an expression of unalloyed rapture, — I should select it from the songs of all the birds I know as the voice of unshadowed gladness.

"OD Almightie first planted a Garden,"
says Lord Bacon. "And indeed it is
the Purest of Humane Pleasures, it is
the Greatest Refreshment to the Spirits of Man."
Never were truer words spoken.

So deeply is the gardener's instinct implanted
in my soul, I really love the tools with which I
work, — the iron fork, the spade, the hoe, the
rake, the trowel, and the watering-pot are pleasant
objects in my eyes. The ingenuity of modern
times has invented many variations of these prim-
itive instruments of toil, and many of them are
most useful and helpful, as, for instance, a short,
five-pronged hand-fork, a delightful tool to use in
breaking up the earth about the roots of weeds.
Some of the weeds are so wide-spreading and
tenacious, like clover and mallow, that they seem
to have fastened themselves around the nether
millstone, it is so difficult to disengage their hold.
Once loosened, however, by the friendly little
fork, they must come up, whether they will or no.

I like to take the hoe in my hands and break

24

to pieces the clods of earth left by the overturn-
ing spade, to work into the soil the dark, velvet-
smooth, scentless barn manure which is to furnish
the best of food for my flowers ; it is a pleasure
to handle the light rake, drawing it evenly through
the soil and combing out every stick and stone
and straw and lump, till the ground is as smooth
and fine as meal. This done carefully and thoroughly, the beds laid out neatly, with their surface level as a floor, and not heaped high enough
to let the rains run off, — then is the ground
ready for the sowing of the seeds.

The very act of planting a seed in the earth
has in it to me something beautiful. I always do
it with a joy that is largely mixed with awe. I
watch my garden beds after they are sown, and
think how one of God's exquisite miracles is
going on beneath the dark earth out of sight. I
never forget my planted seeds. Often I wake in
the night and think how the rains and the dews
have reached to the dry shell and softened it; how
the spirit of life begins to stir within, and the in-
dividuality of the plant to assert itself ; how it is
thrusting two hands forth from the imprisoning
husk, one, the root, to grasp the earth, to hold
itself firm and absorb its food, the other stretching above to find the light, that it may drink in
the breeze and sunshine and so climb to its full
perfection of beauty. It is curious that the leaf
should so love the light and the root so hate it.
In his " Proserpina " John Ruskin discourses on
this subject in his own inimitable way. All he
says of this is most interesting and suggestive :

"The first instinct of the stem, . . . the instinct
of seeking the light, as of the root to seek darkness — what words can speak the wonder of it?"
If "the seed falls in the ground with the springing germ of it downwards, with heavenly cunning
the taught stem curls round and seeks the never
seen light." The "taught" stem! Who taught
it? What he says of the leaves and stems is very
beautiful; every one should read it. I really do
not know which is most wonderful of these de-
scriptions of his, but nothing could be more striking than this definition: "A root is a group of
growing fibres which taste and suck what is good
for the plant out of the ground, and by their
united strength hold it in its place. . . . The thick
limbs of roots do not feed, but only the fine ends
of them, which are something between tongues
and sponges, and while they absorb moisture
readily, are yet as particular about getting what
they think nice to eat as any dainty little boy or
girl; looking for it everywhere, and turning
angry and sulky if they don't get it."

There could not be a better description than
this, and if any seedsman would like to make his
fortune without delay, he has only to have printed
on every packet of seed he offers for sale the
kind of soil, the food, required by each plant.
For instance, why not say of Mignonette, It flour-
ishes best in a poor and sandy soil; so treated it
is much more fragrant than in a rich earth, which
causes it to run to leaves and makes its flowers
fewer and less sweet. Or of Poppies, Plant them
in a rich sandy loam, all except the Californias

(*Eschscholtzia*), which do best in a poor soil. Or of Pansies, Give them the richest earth you can find, no end of water, and partial shade. Or, Don't worry over drought for your Nasturtiums; they come from Chile and will live and thrive with less water than almost anything else that grows; don't trouble yourself to enrich the ground for them; that makes them profuse and coarse of leaves and sparing of flowers; leave them to shift for themselves, once having cleared them of weeds. No flower bears neglect so well. Or, Give your Zinnias a heavy soil; they like clay. Or, Keep Sweet Peas as wet as you can and make the ground for them as rich as possible. Or, Keep barn manure away from your Lilies for your life! they will not brook contact with it, but a rich soil they also like, only it must be made so by anything rather than stable manure, and they, too, like clay; they blossom best when it is given them. But transport to your garden a portion of the very barnyard itself in which to set Roses, Sunflowers and Hollyhocks, Honeysuckles and Dahlias. Hints of this kind would be to the unaccustomed tiller of the soil simply invaluable. How much they would lessen failures and discouragements! And to learn these things by one's self takes half a lifetime of sad experience.

To return to our planting. Yes, the sowing of a seed seems a very simple matter, but I always feel as if it were a sacred thing among the mysteries of God. Standing by that space of blank and motionless ground, I think of all it holds for me of beauty and delight, and I am filled with

joy at the thought that I may be the magician to
whom power is given to summon so sweet a pa-
geant from the silent and passive soil. I bring a
mat from the house and kneel by the smooth bed
of mellow brown earth, lay a narrow strip of board
across it a few inches from one end, draw a furrow firmly and evenly in the ground along the
edge of the board, repeating this until the whole
bed is grooved at equal distances across its entire
length. Into these straight furrows the living
seeds are dropped, the earth replaced over them
(with a depth of about twice their diameter), and
the board laid flat with gentle pressure over all
the surface till it is perfectly smooth again. Then
must the whole be lightly and carefully watered.
With almost all the seeds sown in this bird-
blest and persecuted little garden, I am obliged
to lay newspapers or some protection over the
planted beds, and over these again sheets of wire
netting, to keep off the singing sparrows till the
seeds are safely sprouted. Last year, one morning early in May, I put a border of Mignonette
seeds round every flower bed. When I came to
the garden again in the afternoon, it was alive
with flirting wings and tails and saucy beaks and
bright eyes, and stout little legs and claws scratch-
ing like mad; all white-throats and song-sparrows, and hardly a seed had these merry little
marauders left in the ground. Around the edge
of each bed a groove ran, nicely hollowed by their
industrious feet, and empty as my hopes. I replaced the seed from my store, and this time took
great pains to lay two laths side by side over the

lines I had sowed, for safety. Next morning I
found the birds again at it; they had burrowed
under, kicked over, scratched away the light
sticks, and again the seeds were all devoured.
Patiently I planted once more, and this time
dragged from a pile of lumber heavy square
beams of different lengths, which I laid along the
borders. The birds eyed the barricades, strove
to burrow under, but were forced to give it up,
and so at last I conquered. In the course of a
week I turned over the protecting beams and
found the little Mignonette plants white as potato
shoots that have sprouted in a cellar, but safe, for
which I was devoutly thankful! A day or two
of sun and air made them green and strong, and
all summer long I valued every fragrant spike of
flowers they gave me, doubly, because of all the
trouble I had gone through to save them. I
mention this little episode merely to illustrate the
fact that the would-be gardener requires more
patience than most mortals!

The state of the weather, the temperature of
the air, the amount of rain which falls, make all
the difference in the world in the time it takes
for the first green leaves to appear. Some seeds
take longer than others to germinate: for instance, Hollyhocks, Marigolds, ten weeks Stocks
or Gillyflowers, Rose of Heaven, Zinnias, and many
others come up in from three to five days if all
circumstances are favorable, that is, if it is warm,
moist, and sunny enough ; Asters, single Dahlias,
Sunflowers, Cornflowers, Mignonette, Coreopsis,
Morning-glory, Picotee Pinks, Wallflowers, Sweet

Williams, and by far the greater number of an-
nuals appear in from five to seven days; Balsams,
Pansies, Begonias, Drummond's Phlox, Poppies,
Verbenas, Thunbergia, and many others, in from
eight to ten days; Columbines, Flax, Artemisia,
Feverfew, Campanula, and so forth, in from ten to
twelve days; Maurandia, Forget-me-not, Petunia,
Lantana, Nicotiana (an exquisite flower, by the
way), in from twelve to fifteen days; Cobœa,
Gloxinia, Primroses, Geraniums, and others, in
from fifteen to twenty days; Perennial Phlox,
Clematis, Perennial Larkspurs (which are
heavenly!), and various others, take from twenty
to thirty-five days to germinate; and as for Lu-
pines and Lilies and Ampelopsis, and the like,
they take a whole year! But common gardeners
don't try to raise these from seed, fortunately.

With the first faint green lines that are visible
along the flower beds come the weeds, yea, and
even before them; a wild, vigorous, straggling
army, full of health, of strength, and a most marvelous power of growth. These must be dealt
with at once and without mercy; they must be
pulled up root and branch, without a moment's
delay. There is clover that appears with a little
circular leaf and has a root that seems to reach
all round in the under world; it goes everywhere
and holds on to the earth with a grip which is
unequaled by anything that grows. Not an atom
of its roots must be left in the ground, for every
thread of it will send up new shoots, and if not
watched fill all the space in a few weeks. Another
difficult weed to manage is the chickweed, which

is so delicate that it breaks at the slightest touch. It is a most all-pervading weed; it fills every space between the flowers, overruns them like a green mist, and will surely strangle them if left unmolested. Alphonse Karr, who so greatly enjoyed his garden, and wrote of it with so much pleasure, says: " The chickweed is endowed with a fecundity that no other plant possesses. . . . Seven or eight generations of chickweed cover the earth every year. . . . It occupies the fields naturally, and invades our gardens; it is almost impossible to destroy it."

There is a long procession of weeds to be fought: pigweed, ragweed, smartweed, shepherd's purse, mallow, mustard, sorrel, and many more, which make the first crop. The second consists largely of quitch-grass, the very worst of all, and purslain or pusley, which Charles Dudley Warner has immortalized in his charming book, " My Summer in a Garden." The roots of quitch-grass are as strong as steel and run rapidly in all directions underneath the surface, sending up tender shoots that break too easily when you touch them. The root must be found, grasped firmly, and followed its whole length to utter extermination, or the grass will come up like a giant, and later cannot be dealt with except by pulling up also the flowers among which it inextricably entangles itself. The flat, olive-green leaves and red. fleshy stems of the pusley, running over the ground in a mat, next appear; this is easily disposed of, only it continues to come up, —fresh plants in endless succession rise from the soil all

summer, and must be watched and faithfully destroyed.

There is one weed, or wild plant, dodder by
name, which has given my island garden the
greatest possible trouble. It is often wrongly
called gold-thread, because it looks like a tangled
mass of amber thread, but the true gold-thread is
quite different. The whole plant consists of nothing but these seemingly endless brittle reddish
yellow stalks with bunches of small, dull, whitish
flowers without stems, borne at intervals, with no
leaves at all. It has no root in the earth, it is a
parasite, and not at all particular as to what it
fastens itself upon; anything that comes in its
way will answer its purpose. It is very pretty in
its place, growing among the goldenrod and blue
skullcap at the top of the rocky little coves that
slope down to the water about the island, throwing itself from plant to plant, and making a mass
of translucent amber color. But alas! when it
gets into a civilized garden, woe, woe unto that
garden! A handful of it in bloom was brought
to my piazza twenty years ago, and some of it
was accidentally thrown into the flower beds; I
have been fighting it ever since. I have never
yet been able to get rid of it! Next year I found
my Nasturtiums, Cornflowers, Marigolds, and all
the rest tangled together in this yellow web, a
mass of inextricable confusion. Year after year
I waged war against it, but even yet it is not entirely exterminated. I never allow a plant of it
in the garden, no seeds of it ripen there, and none
of it grows near the place outside; not a single

atom of it in my small domain could possibly escape my eye, and yet its seeds come up more or
less every year; I am sure to find one or two
plants of it in the garden somewhere. They
emerge from the ground, each like a fine yellow
hair, till they are an inch and a half or two inches
long; they reach with might and main toward
the nearest legitimate growing plant, and when
they touch it cling to it like a limpet; then they
draw their other end up out of the ground and
set up housekeeping for the rest of their lives.
They adhere to the unhappy individual upon
which they have fixed themselves with a grip that
grows more and more horrible; they suck all its
juices, drink all its health and strength and
beauty, and fling out trailers to the next and the
next and the next, till the whole garden is a mass
of ruin and despair.

For many springs after the first year it appeared I used to take a glass tumbler and go all
over the beds soon after they were laid out, pulling up these tiny yellow hairs, and in an hour or
two I have pulled up five or six tumblers full. I
gathered them in glasses so that I might be quite
sure of all I plucked, and because they could not
easily blow away out of such a receptacle. For
wherever they might fall, if they touched a green
growing thing they would in an astonishingly
short space of time make themselves fast for
good, or rather for ill! Every year I watch for it
with the most eager vigilance as I weed carefully
over the whole surface of the little pleasance,
but sometimes it steals up after all the weeding

is done, and, before I know it, I find it has begun to tie the flowers together. Then I pull up all the plants it has touched, lay them in a basket, carry them down, and cast the whole into the sea. It is the only way to be rid of it. I have known it wind its inexorable way tightly up the large smooth stem of a tall Sunflower, where I had not thought of looking for it, till there was not an atom of the skin of the stalk visible, only amber-colored dodder and its white, dull flowers from the great head of the blossoming Sunflower tree to its root. Into the sea the whole thing went, at once, without a moment of delay!

These are only a few of the weeds with which one must battle, though dodder, I fancy, seldom troubles any one on the planet as it does me. It takes an island garden to produce so remarkable a growth! Most of them soon become familiar, too familiar, indeed, and at last one learns how to manage them. The great mistake which the inexperienced gardener makes is in leaving a morsel of the root of a weed in the ground. Only by combing the earth through and through between the rows of plants with the small hand-fork (after all the intruders have been removed as carefully as possible with the hand), can you be sure that they are gone. Other seeds of weeds will be overturned and brought to the surface in the process, and these will sprout in their turn, but by this time the flowers will have made so much headway that they will crowd out the new crop of weeds enough to insure their own safety, except in some few instances. Apple of Peru

(Stramonium) is one of the most powerful and
persistent among the enemies; a poisonous thing
with a loathsome odor, it must be watched for
and routed, which fortunately is easily done. In
its perfected growth this is the most uncanny
plant, — a strong, low bush with bat-like leaves
of dark green, and long, pale lavender, lily-like
flowers, followed by a round spiked seed-vessel.
Says Hawthorne: "What hidden virtue is in
these things that it is granted to sow themselves
with the wind and to grapple the earth with this
immitigable stubbornness, and to flourish in spite
of obstacles, and never to suffer blight beneath
any sun or shade, but always to mock their enemies with the same wicked luxuriance?" Mrs.
Gatty (the mother of that beautiful woman,
Juliana Horatia Ewing, who has so discoursed on
the subject of flowers and many other things as
to make all time her debtor) answers the question, "What is a weed?" by this statement, "A
weed is a plant out of place." A keen and close
observer of nature says: "A better definition
would be, ' A plant which has an innate disposi-
tion to *get* into the wrong place;'" and goes on
to say: "This is the very essence of weed character — in plants as in men. If you glance through
your botanical books you will see often added to
certain names, 'a troublesome weed.' It is not
its being venomous or ugly, but its being imper-
tinent — thrusting itself where it has no business
and hinders other people's business — that makes
a weed of it. . . . Who ever saw a wood anemone
or a heath blossom out of place? . . . What is it,

then, this temper in some plants — malicious as it seems, intrusive, at all events, or erring — which brings them out of their places, thrusts them where they thwart us and offend?" This seems to me the best definition of what constitutes a weed that I have seen.

And their strength is mighty, and their name is legion. If there were no other enemies which the gardener must fight, this one of weeds alone is quite enough to tax all his powers and patience.

Then the plants kill each other if they are left to grow as thickly together as the seeds were sown; they must be "thinned out" as soon as they have attained to their second leaf, leaving two, three, four, or five inches between each two plants side by side. I always leave two plants where one would be enough, because something is so likely to happen to destroy them, and if there are two the hard fates may perhaps leave one. Some things require much more space than others. Pinks that spire up so thin and tall can be set closer together than Poppies, which spread widely in all directions. This pulling up and throwing away of the superfluous plants is a very difficult thing for me to do. I cannot bear to destroy one of the precious young seedlings that I have watched and tended with such love and care, but it must be done. It is a matter of the very greatest importance. The welfare of the garden depends on it. I comfort myself as best I may by saving all that will bear transplanting, and then giving them away to the flower plots of my fellow-gardeners on neighboring islands.

Soon the whole plot mantles over all its surface with the rich, warm green of vigorous leaf-
age. The new growth rejoices. That is the
right word for it. The gladness of green growing
things is apparent to any seeing eye. They rejoice with a radiant joy in sun and rain and air
and dew, in all care and kindness. They know
and respond to everything that is done for them.
The low-growing Drummond's Phlox is one of
the most satisfactory flowers for a beginner in the
art of gardening. There is no such word as fail
in its bright lexicon; and it blossoms continually
from the last of June till frost. Looking carefully every day, by the last half of June I find the
pale clustered flower buds showing; then it is
not long to wait before the whole bed is a blaze
of varied color, a delicate woven carpet of myriad
vivid hues. In the lovely buds the petals are
folded one over the other in beautiful succession.
The flowers are five-petaled, with a faint, sweet
perfume; they are borne in flat clusters of an
exquisite, velvety texture, with a clearly marked
eye in the centre encircling the few pearl-white
stamens; this eye varies with the hue of each
different flower. There will be delicious pinks
among these Phloxes, from the palest rose to the
deepest cherry; all shades of red from bright,
light scarlet, clear and pure, to a rich black red, —
the Black Warrior. There will be all heavenly
purples, pale lilacs, deep red purple and blue
purple, perfect snow white: the eye in this last is
soft green, like the touches on a Snowdrop bell.
The scarlet flowers have a ring of black-red about

the centre, delicately gorgeous. There are almost
endless varieties and mixtures of color; they are
full of surprises. The Star of Quedlinburg is
such a pretty, quaint change rung upon this
pleasant theme of Phloxes. The centre of the
outer line of each petal is drawn out at the edge
like the tails on the under wings of the Luna
moth. These long tails in which each petal ter-
minates give the flower the aspect of a star with
rays. "Ask of Nature why the star form she
repeats," says Emerson. It is forever repeated
among the flowers.

At bird-peep, as the country folk have a charming way of calling the break of day, I am in my
dear garden, — planting and transplanting, hoeing,
raking, weeding, watering, tying up and training
those plants that need it, and always fighting for
their precious lives against their legions of enemies. There is a time of great danger upon the
island from the birds when they are migrating
northward. They come suddenly down from the
sky in myriads, on their way to the continent,
and I have known them to strip the little plot of
every green shoot in a single day, utterly bare.
Nothing but fishing nets draped over the whole
space will save the garden when these hungry
hordes descend. But I do not lose patience with
the birds, however sorely they try me. I love
them too well. How should they know that the
garden was not planted for them? Those be-
longing to the thrush tribe are the most mis-
chievous; the others do not disturb the flower
beds so much. The friendly robin, though a

The Garden in its Glory

Celia Thaxter on her piazza.

thrush, only comes for worms, to which he is
more than welcome. Most of the other birds —
bobolinks, kingbirds, orioles, purple finches, and
many other beautiful creatures less familiar —
stay with us for a short time only, on their passage north or south every year; but a single pair
of kingbirds build every summer in the one tall
elm-tree on the island, where also builds a cosy
nuthatch and raises a numerous family, and one
pair of most interesting kingfishers haunts the
upper cove till late in the season. A Maryland
yellow-throat began building here last summer.
For several years one pair of cuckoos lingered
through the summer, but at last ceased to come.
A few blackbirds build, the white-throats stay
late, but several varieties of swallows, the song-
sparrows, and sandpipers remain and rear their
broods. How we wish the robins would stay too,
and the orioles and all the sweet company! But
there are no trees to shelter them. Their coming
and going, however, is a matter of the greatest
interest to the little family on the island, and we
are thrown into a state of the deepest excitement
by the apparition of a scarlet tanager, or a rose-
breasted grosbeak, or any of those unfamiliar
beauties. Once a ferruginous thrush came and
stayed a week with us in early June. Every day
when he perched on a ridge-pole or chimney-top
and sang, the whole family turned out in a body
to listen, making a business of it, attending to nothing else while that thrilling melody was poured
out on the silent air. That was a gift of the gods
which we could, none of us, afford to neglect!

Says the wise Lord Bacon again: "And because the Breath of Flowers is far sweeter in the
Aire (when it comes and goes, like the Warbling
of Music) than in the hand, therefore nothing is
more fit for that delight than to know what be
the Flowers and Plants that doe best perfume the
Aire."

The most exquisite perfume known to my garden is that of the Wallflowers; there is nothing
equal to it. They blossom early, and generally
before June has passed they are gone, and have
left me mourning their too swift departure. I
wonder they are not more generally cultivated,
but I fancy the fact that they do not blossom till
the second year has much to do with their rarity.
It requires so much more faith and patience to
wait a whole year, and meanwhile carefully watch
and tend the plants, excepting during the time
when winter covers them with a blanket of snow;
but when at last spring comes and the tardy
flowers appear, then one is a thousand times re-
paid for all the tedious months of waiting. They
return such wealth of bloom and fragrance for
the care and thought bestowed on them! Their
thick spikes of velvet blossoms are in all shades
of rich red, from scarlet to the darkest brown,
from light gold to orange; some are purple; and
their odor, — who shall describe it! Violets,
Roses, Lilies, Sweet Peas, Mignonette, and Helio-
trope, with a dash of Honeysuckle, all mingled
in a heavenly whole. There is no perfume which
I know that can equal it. And they are so lavish
of their scent; it is borne off the garden and

wafted everywhere, into the house and here and
there in all directions, in viewless clouds on the
gentle air. To make a perfect success of Wallflowers they must be given lime in some form
about the roots. They thrive marvelously if fed
with a mixture of old plastering in the soil, or
bone meal, or, if that is not at hand, the meat
bones from the kitchen, calcined in the oven and
pounded into bits, stirred in around the roots is
fine for them. This treatment makes all the difference in the world in their strength and beauty.
After the Wallflowers, Roses and Lilies, Mignonette, Pinks, Gillyflowers, Sweet Peas, and the
Honeysuckles for fragrance, and of these last, the
monthly Honeysuckle is the most divine. Such
vigor of growth I have never seen in any other
plant, and it is hardy even without the least protection in our northern climate. It climbs the
trellis on my piazza and spreads its superb clusters of flowers from time to time all summer.
Each cluster is a triumph of beauty, flat in the
centre and curving out to the blossoming edge in
joyous lines of loveliness, most like a wreath of
heavenly trumpets breathing melodies of perfume
to the air. Each trumpet of lustrous white
deepens to a yellower tint in the centre where the
small ends meet; each blossom where it opens at
the lip is tipped with fresh pink; each sends out
a group of long stamens from its slender throat
like rays of light; and the whole circle of radiant
flowers has an effect of gladness and glory indescribable : the very sight of it lifts and refreshes
the human heart. And for its odor, it is like the

spirit of romance, sweet as youth's tender dreams.
It is summer's very soul.

This beautiful vine will grow anywhere, for anybody, only give it half a chance, such is its matchless vigor.   I wonder why it is not found in every
garden ; nothing so well repays the slightest care.

Next in power come the Sweet Peas, blossoming
the livelong summer in all lovely tints save only
yellow, and even that the kind called Primrose
approaches, with its faint gold suffusion of both
inner and outer petals.   I plant them by myriads
in my tiny garden — all it will hold.   Transplant,
I should say, because of my friends the birds, who
never leave me one if I dare plant them out of
doors.   But this transplanting is most delightful.
I thoroughly enjoy digging with the hoe a long
trench six inches deep for the strong young seedlings, lifting them from the boxes, carefully disen-
tangling their long white roots each from the other
as I take them out, and placing them in a close
row the whole length of the deep furrow, letting
the roots drop their whole length, with no curling
or crowding, then half filling the hollow with
water, drawing the earth about the roots and
firming the whole with strong and gentle touch.
They do not droop a single leaf so transplanted ;
they go on growing as if nothing had happened,
if only they are given all the water they need.
Already they stretch out their delicate tendrils to
climb, and I love to give them for support the
sticks with which the farmers supply their pea
vines for the market; but on my island are no
woods, so I am thankful for humble bayberry and

elder branches for the purpose. It is another
pleasure to go afar among the rocks for these and
wheel them to the flower beds in a light wheelbarrow, which is one of the most useful things
one can possess for work about the garden. At
once the vines lay hold of the slender sticks and
climb to the very top, fain are they to go much
farther. But I cut the tops so that they may
branch from the sides and keep within bounds,
and they soon make a solid hedge of healthy
green. Oh, when the blossoms break from these
green hedges like heavenly winged angels, and
their pure, cool perfume fills the air, what joy is
mine!

I find Sweet Peas can hardly have too rich a
soil, provided always that they are kept sufficiently
wet. They *must* have moisture, their roots must
be kept cool and damp, — a mulch of leaves or
straw is a very good thing to keep the roots from
drying, — and they must always be planted as deep
as possible. Wood ashes give them a stronger
growth. Their colors, the great variety of them,
and their vivid delicacy are wonderful; they are
most beautiful against the background of the sea;
they are a continual source of delight, and never
cease to bloom, with me, if gathered every day and
watered abundantly, the whole summer long, even
through the autumn till November. But they
must never be suffered to go to seed; that would
check their blossoming at once. I revel in their
beauty week after week, bringing them into the
house and arranging them in masses every other
day. Clear glass vases are most effective for

them, and they look loveliest, I think, when each color is kept by itself. For the Princess Beatrice, which is a divine pale pink, a shade of rose refined and exquisite, there are glasses of clear pink that repeat the hues of the flowers with magical gradations and reflections. For the white kinds there are white vases, the most effective of ground glass, the opaque surface of which matches the tone of the flowers.

Of the named kinds of Sweet Peas the most beautiful shades of pink that I know are the divinely delicate Princess Beatrice, the palest rose-color; Adonis, a deeper pink, very clear and rich; the Orange Prince, a most ineffably splendid color of bright yellow-rose; these together make a combination of color that satisfies the inmost soul. Carmine Invincible is the most splendid red; the Butterfly is white edged with mauve, and combined with the delicate rose Princess Beatrice makes a delicious harmony. Blanche Ferry is also a lovely rose. Queen Victoria is the best white I have known; but every year new varieties are found which seem more and more beautiful, and it is only by trying them that one finds which to depend on.

Of the worth of these I have mentioned I am sure; they are the strongest growers, the freest bloomers, and the most beautiful of their kind. They never disappoint you if you give them the right care. The list of flowers in my island garden is by no means long, but I could discourse of them forever! They are mostly the old-fashioned flowers our grandmothers loved. Beginning with

Snowdrops, Crocuses, Daffodils, Narcissus, a few Hyacinths, Scillas, an English Primrose or two, Tulips, and several other early blooming plants, one big red Peony, Columbine, Ragged Robin, Cornflowers, Roses and Lilies, Larkspurs, Pinks and Gillyflowers, Sweet Williams, Wallflowers, Forget-me-nots, single Dahlias, Sunflowers of every kind, and Hollyhocks of all colors, Poppies in almost endless variety, Nasturtiums of all hues, pot Marigolds, summer Chrysanthemums in great variety, Rose Campion, or Rose of Heaven, Pansies, Phlox, Sweet Peas, and Mignonette, Crimson Flax and the tall blue Perennial Flax (a wonderful blue!), many kinds of Coreopsis, — all most valuable and decorative, — Asters, Honeysuckle and Clematis, Morning-glories, Lavender and Foxgloves, Candytuft, Verbenas, Thunbergia, Pentstemon, the heaven-blue Ipomea, white Petunias, — because they are so beautiful by moonlight, — a few Four-o'clocks, and so forth. These are enough for a most happy little garden. A few more modern plants are added, a golden and a rosy Lily from Japan, a lustrous white gold-hearted Anemone from the same country, for autumn blooming, one or two tuberous-rooted Begonias, some Gaillardias and Zinnias, the fragrant little Asperula (Woodruff), and some others. Among the new plants one of the most interesting is the Hugelia Cœrulea, which grows a foot and a half high, with a many-branched woolly leaf, and flowers in flat clusters of the most delicious light blue. This is a flower with an atmosphere; it has a quality of beauty quite indescribable.

COPY the notes of a few days' work in the garden in May, just to give an idea of their character and of the variety of occupation in this small space of ground.

May 11. This morning at four o'clock the sky was one rich red blush in the east, over a sea as calm as a mirror. How could I wait for the sun to lift its scarlet rim above the dim sea-line (though it rose punctually at forty-seven minutes past four), when my precious flower beds were waiting for me! It was not possible, and I was up and dressed before he had flooded the earth with glory. "Straight was a path of gold for him," I said, as I gazed out at the long line of liquid splendor along the ocean. All the boxes and baskets of the more delicate seedlings were to be put out from my chamber window on flat house-top and balcony, they and the forest of Sweet Peas to be thoroughly watered, and the Pansies half shaded with paper lest the sun should work them woe. At five the household was stirring, there was time to write a letter or two, then came breakfast before six, and by half past six I was out of doors at work in the vast

46

circle of motionless silence, for the sea was too
calm for me to hear even its breathing. It was
so beautiful, — the dewy quiet, the freshness, the
long, still shadows, the matchless, delicate, sweet
charm of the newly wakened world. Such a
color as the grass had taken on during the last
few warm days; and where the early shadows lay
long across it, such indescribable richness of
tone! There was so much for me to do, I hardly
knew where to begin. At the east of the house
the bed of Pansies set out yesterday was bright
with promise, every little plant holding itself
gladly erect. I began with the trellis each side of
the steps leading down into the garden, and first
set out a Cobœa Scandens, one to the right and
one to the left, — strong, sturdy plants which I
had been keeping weeks in the house till it should
be warm enough to trust them out of doors.
They were a foot high and stretching their sensitive tendrils in all directions, seeking something
for support. They grasped the trellis at once
and seemed to spread out every leaf to the warm
sun, while I poured cool water and liquid manure
about their roots, and congratulated them on their
escape into the open ground. Near them, against
the same trellis, I put down two Tropæolum Lob-
bianum Lucifers, a new scarlet variety of these
delicate Nasturtiums, that they might climb together over the broad arch. Some time ago I had
planted there also some Mexican Morning-glories
sent me by an unknown friend, and if they come
up, and Cobœa, Nasturtiums, and Morning-glories
all climb together and clasp hands with Honey-

suckle, Wistaria, and Wild Cucumber, my porch
will, indeed, be a bower of beauty! Then against
wall and fence I set out the stout bushes of single
Dahlias which have been growing ever since last
January. A new variety called Star of Lyons interests me. I am anxious to know what it is like,
what its color, what its shape. It is such a pleasure always to be finding new varieties and combinations, fresh surprises in unfamiliar flowers.
Seeking the smallest posy bed I own, into this I
transplanted another stranger, Papaver Alpinum
Roseum, a rose-colored Iceland Poppy. How I
shall watch it grow, and how eagerly wait for it
to blossom! Eight egg-shells full of it were set
down and carefully watered. Next, a row of
baby Wallflowers were established in a long line
near the tall ones that are thick with buds. I
am going to try to have a succession of bloom
from these, if it can be accomplished, all summer.
In another bed I began to set out a few of the
choicest Sweet Peas, the new kinds; these were
already a foot long from tip to root ends. I have
no words to tell what pleasant work this is!
After the Sweet Peas were comfortably settled, I
covered the whole bed with a length of light
mosquito net, pegging it at the corners, laying
sticks and stones along the edges to hold it down,
so that the saucy sparrows should find no loophole by which to wriggle inside, they having
watched the whole process with interested eyes
from their perch on the fence-rail. How beautiful it was to be sitting there in the sweet weather,
working in the wholesome brown earth! Just be-

yond the Sweet Peas I could see my strong white
Lilies springing up, a foot high already, with the
splendid hardy Larkspurs behind them, prom-
ising a wealth of white and gold and azure by
and by. From time to time through the calm
morning, as I labored thus peacefully, I heard the
loons laughing loud and clear in the stillness,
and by lifting my head could see them off the
end of the wharf at the landing swimming to and
fro with their bright reflections, catching no end
of fish and having the most delightful time, —
every now and then half raising themselves from
the water and flapping their wings, showing the
dazzling white with which the strong pinions
were lined, and laughing again and again with a
wild and eerie sound. This means that a storm
is coming, I know. But I love to hear them, and
how devoutly thankful I am that there is not a
creature with a gun on this blessed island! The
loons know it well, or they never would venture
in so near, while they shout to the morning their
wild cries.

Near me, where I had made the earth so very
wet, suddenly fluttered down a ruddy-breasted
barn swallow, the beauty! for on such heavenly
terms are we that he did not mind me in the
least as he gathered a tiny load of mud for his
nest against the rafters in the barn, and flew away
with it low on the wind. The barn swallows do
not visit my small inclosure as often as do my
nearer neighbors, the white-breasted martins.

All this time the lovely day was slowly changing its early delicate colors and freshness for the

whiter light of noon. By twelve o'clock the wind
had "hauled" from west to south, going round
through the east, and sending millions of light
ripples across the glassy water, deepening its
color to sparkling sapphire, and at last the sun
overhead seemed to pelt quicksilver in floods
upon it, and then it was dinner-time. After an
hour of rest again I took up my work. All
about, here and there and everywhere, I dug up
the scattered Echinocystus vines and set them
against the house, so that they could run up the
trellises on all sides to make grateful shade by
and by. A few straying Primroses waited to be
moved outside the fence, — they take up so much
room within, and room is so precious inside the
garden. Young plants of the charming, old-fashioned Sweet Rocket had to be collected from the
nooks where they had sown themselves far and
near, and set in clumps in corners. Then there
was a box of white Forget-me-nots some one had
sent me, to be established in their places, and I
finished the afternoon by planting Shirley Poppies all up and down the large bank at the southwest of the garden, outside. I am always planting
Shirley Poppies somewhere! One never can
have enough of them, and by putting them into
the ground at intervals of a week, later and later,
one can secure a succession of bloom and keep
them for a much longer time, — keep, indeed, their
heavenly beauty to enjoy the livelong summer, —
whereas, if they are all planted at once you would
see them for a blissful moment, a week or ten
days at most, and then they are gone. I have

Larkspurs and Lilies

Artist Childe Hassam at work on Celia's piazza.

planted and am going to continue planting till the middle of June, in this year of grace 1893, no less than two whole ounces of Shirley Poppies in all, and when one reflects that the seeds are so small as to be hardly more than visible to the naked eye, one realizes this to be a great many.

May 12th. Again a radiant day. I watched the thin white half ring of the waning moon as it stole up the east through the May haze at dawn. This kind of haze belongs especially to this month; it is such an exquisite color, like ashes of roses, till the sun suffuses it with a burning blush before he leaps alive from the ocean's rim. Again in the garden at a little after six, to find the sparrows busy tunneling up and down the bank, devouring the Poppies that I planted yesterday. How they can see the seeds at all, or why they should care to feast on anything so small, or why they do not all perish, as poor Pillicoddy proposed doing, from the effects of such doses of opium, passes my understanding. There was nothing to be done but to plant them all over and then trail through the dewy grass long boards to lay up and down, covering the bank, for protection.

First, there were the small Tea Rosebushes to be set out in their sunny bed, made rich with finely sifted manure and soot and a sprinkling of wood ashes. And here let me say that all through the spring, beginning when the hardy Damask and Jacqueminots, etc., are just unfolding their leaf buds, it is a most excellent plan to sift wood ashes quite thickly over all the Rose-

bushes, either just after a shower or after you
have been sprinkling them; let it remain on
them for several hours, — if the sun is not shining
I leave it half a day, — but then it must all be
carefully washed off, every trace of it, or it will
spoil the leaves. This kills or discourages all
sorts of insect pests, and the effect of the ashes
on the soil about their roots is most beneficial to
the Roses.

As I sat in measureless content by the little
flower bed, carefully slipping my pretty Bon
Silenes and Catherine Mermets and yellow Sun-
sets and the rest out of their pots, and gently
firming them in the ground, with plenty of water
for refreshment, a cloud of the most delicious
perfume brooded about me from a bed of white
violets at the left, the hardiest, faithfulest, friend-
liest little flowers in the world. I found two
small Polyantha Roses had lived all winter in this
sheltered bed; that was indeed a charming find!
At the back of it grows a tall Jacqueminot, a
black Tuscany Rose, and the strong white Rosa
Rugosa, a Japanese variety which bears very
large single flowers in the greatest profusion.
This Rose is extremely valuable, easily obtained,
so hardy as to be almost indestructible, and absolutely untroubled by any disease or insect plague
whatever. Its foliage is always fresh and handsome, and its seed vessels are huge scarlet balls
as large as an average Crab-Apple, most ornamen-
tal after the flowers are gone. But the old, old
black Tuscany Rose is the most precious of all.
Mine came from an ancient garden that vanished

long ago, but which used to be a glory to the
town in which it grew. It is a hardy Rose also,
in color so darkly red as to be almost black, —a
warm red, less crimson than scarlet, glowing with
a kind of smouldering splendor, with only two
rows of petals round a centre of richest gold.
At the end of this bed is a Water Hyacinth floating in its tub, and near it, in another tub, a large
pink Water Lily, kept over from last summer in
a frost-proof cellar, is sending up the loveliest
leaves, touched with so sweet a crimson as to be
almost as delightful as the blossoms themselves.
All the rest of this day was spent in transplanting
Asters from boxes into the beds all over the garden, edging nearly every bed with them, so that
when the fleeting glory of Poppies and other earlier annuals is gone there will still be beautiful
color to gladden our eyes late in the summer,
quite into the autumn days.

In the afternoon I had all the many boxes of
Sweet Peas brought to the piazza to be ready for
transplanting, but remembering the sparrows, I
covered each box carefully with mosquito netting
before leaving them for the night.

14th. Sunday. A storm of wild wind and
flooding rain, the storm the loons predicted! At
breakfast my gardening brother said, "Well, my
sweet peas are all gone!" "Oh," I cried in
the greatest sympathy, "what has happened to
them?" for he had planted six pounds or more,
and they had come up finely. "Sparrows," was
his laconic reply. I flew to my boxes on the
piazza: they were safe, only through a tiny crack

in the net over one a bird had wriggled its little
body, and pulled up and flung the plants to right
and left all over the steps. But my brother's long
rows, so green last night, were bare except for
broken stems and withering leaves. Alas, it is so
much trouble to cover such a large area with netting, he thought this time he would trust to luck,
or Providence, or whatever one chooses to call it,
but it is a fatal thing to do. Now he has to
plant all over again, even though I shall share my
boxes with him, and it will make his garden very
late indeed. This time he will not fail to put
nets over all! I sat on the piazza sheltered from
the rain and watched the birds. Unmindful of
the tempest, they skipped gayly round the garden,
over and round the steps, examined all the tucked
up boxes of Sweet Peas, wished they could get in,
but finding it out of the question gave it up and
resigned themselves to the inevitable. To and
fro, here and there they went, peering into every
nook and corner, behind every leaf and stick and
board and stalk, busily pecking away and devouring something with the greatest industry. I
drew nearer to discover what it could be, and to
my great joy found it was the slugs which the
rain had called forth from their hiding-places;
the birds were working the most comprehensive
slaughter among them. At that pleasing sight
I forgave them on the spot all their trespasses
against me.

15th. A thick fog wrapped the world in dim-
ness early this morning; at eight o'clock it was
rolling off and piling itself in glorious headlands

over the coast, gleaming snow white in the sun,
but here and there thin silver strips lay across
distant sails and islands, lingering as if loath to
leave the earth for the sky. I took the baskets
of plants I had found necessary to dig up to give
the rest room, and paddled across to the next
island in a little lapstreaked dory, to give them
to my neighbors for their flower plots. Great is
the pleasure in the giving and the taking. It was
such a heavenly morning, so blue and calm after
the tumult of yesterday! Along the far-off coast
the joyous hills seemed laughing in the sunshine,
and the great sea rippled all over with smiles.

From the low shores of the islands came the
singing of the birds over the still water, with an
indescribably quiet and peaceful effect, and as I
rowed into the cove of my destination, passing
the coasts of the little island called Malaga, I saw
outlined against the sky the lovely grasses already blossoming among the rocks. A kingbird
sat on a bowlder and meditated; there was no tree,
so he was fain to be content with a rock to sit on.
I passed him almost near enough to touch him
with my oar, but he did not stir, not he! My
errand done and the plants distributed, I hastened
back to my own dear little plot again, and up and
down all the paths I went, digging out every
unwelcome root of grass, plantain, mallow, cat-
nip, clover, and the rest, once more raking them
clear and clean. Outside, in a bed by itself, I
sunk four pots of repotted Chrysanthemums, to
be ready for the windows in early winter. All
along the piazza are the house plants waiting to

be attended to, cut back, repotted, and the soil enriched for winter blooming. Every day I attend to them, a few at a time. I cannot spare much time from my planting, weeding, watering, transplanting, and so forth, in the garden, but soon they will be all done. Began to transplant a few of the hundreds of the main body of Sweet Pea plants into the ground, carefully covering each bed as I finished with breadths of light mosquito netting to make them sparrow-proof. As I was working busily I heard the sweet calling of curlews, and looking up saw six of them wheeling overhead. Such sociable birds! They replied to my challenge as if I had been one of themselves, and as long as their calls were answered, lingered near, but being forgotten presently drifted off on the wind, their clear whistle sounding fainter and fainter as they were lost in the distance. All the rest of this day was spent in setting out Sweet Peas, and it will take more than a whole day more to finish, for I put them all round against the fence outside, and into every space I can spare for them within. After tea I hunted slugs as usual, and scattered ashes and lime, but I really feel that my friends the toads have done me the inestimable favor of reducing their hideous numbers, for certainly there are less than last year so far. Early in April, as I was vigorously hoeing in a corner, I unearthed a huge toad, to my perfect delight and satisfaction; he had lived all winter, he had doubtless fed on slugs all the autumn. I could have kissed him on the spot! Very carefully I placed him in the middle of a

large green clump of tender Columbine. He
really was n't more than half awake, after his long
winter nap, but he was alive and well, and when
later I went to look after him, lo ! he had crept
off, perhaps to snuggle into the earth once more
for another nap, till the sun should have a little
more power.

To our great joy the frogs that we imported
last year are also alive. We heard the soft rippling
of their voices with the utmost pleasure ; it is a
lovely liquid-sweet sound. They have not lived
over a winter here before. We feared that the
vicinity of so much salt water might be injurious
to them, but this year they have survived, and
perhaps they may be established for good.

May 20th. All the past days have been filled
with transplanting and the most vigorous weeding. In these five days the Sweet Peas have
grown so tall I was obliged to go after sticks for
them to-day, wheeling my light wheelbarrow up
over the hill and across the island toward the
south, where among the old ruined walls of cel-
lars and houses, and little, almost erased garden
plots, the thick growth of Bayberry and Elder
offered me all the sticks I needed. Such a charming business was this ! So beautiful the narrow
road all the way, bordered by the lovely Shadbush in bridal white, the delicate red Cherry with
flowers so like Hawthorn as to be frequently mis-
taken for it, the pink Chokecherry, the common
Wild Cherry (which seems to attract to itself most
of the caterpillars in the land), all blossoming for
dear life, and among thickets of Blackberry, Rasp-

berry, Gooseberry, Wild Currant, Winterberry,
Spirea, and I know not what, such crowds of flowers! The last of the gay golden Erythroniums, the
Dogtooth Violets, dancing in the breeze; the large,
softly colored Anemones, now nearing their end;
the banks of pearly Eyebrights; the white Violets,
lowly and fragrant; the straw-colored Uvularia;
the ivory spikes of Solomon's Seal, just breaking
into bloom, with its companion, the starry Trien-
talis; the tufts of Fern in cool clefts of rocks, — of
these I gathered several clumps for my fernery in
the shade of the piazza. It would take too long
to tell of all the flowers I saw, but one more I
must mention. At the upper edge of a little cove
at the southwest, where the old settlement of more
than a hundred years ago was thickest, the earth
was blue with the pretty Gill-go-over-the-ground,
its charming blossoms covering the green turf and
cropping out among the loose stones, — a dear,
quaint little flower in two shades of blue marked
with rich red-purple. It was too early for the
Pimpernel to be in bloom, but the pink Herb
Robert was out, the smallest of all the Geranium
family, and I saw ranks of Goldenrod more than a
foot high getting ready for autumn. To tell all I
saw and all I loved and rejoiced in would take a
whole day. Oh, the green and brown and golden
mosses, the lovely, lowly growths along the way,
and oh, the birds that sang and the waves that
leaped and murmured along the shore! The
sweet sky and the soft clouds, the far sails, the
full joy of the summer morning, who shall tell
it? I was so happy trundling home my barrow

load of sticks piled to toppling, and finally tip-
ping it up at the garden gate! It took the whole
afternoon to stick the Peas, and I enjoyed every
moment of it. Before putting the dry brittle
branches in the ground, with a small, light hoe I
went all over and through the earth about the
Sweet Peas, uprooting chickweed and clover, pigweed and dogfennel, till there was not a weed to
be seen near them. When night fell I had only
just finished this pleasant work.

21st. Weeding all day in the hot sun; hard
work, but pleasant. I find it the best way to lay
two boards down near the plot I have to weed,
and on them spread a waterproof, or piece of carpet, and kneeling or half reclining on this, get my
face as close to my work as possible. Sitting flat
on these boards, I weed all within my reach, then
roll up a bit of carpet not bigger than a flat-iron
holder, put it at the edge of the space I have
cleared, and lean my elbow on it; that gives me
another arm's-length that I can reach over, and
so I go on till all is done. I move the rest for my
elbow here and there as needed among the flowers. It takes me longer to weed than most people, because I will do it so thoroughly. It is
such a pleasure and satisfaction to clear the beautiful brown earth, smooth and soft, from these
rough growths, leaving the beautiful green Poppies and Larkspurs and Pinks and Asters, and
the rest, in undisturbed possession! Now come
the potent heats that preface summer, and everything grows and expands so fast, the process of
thinning the crowded plants must begin forth-

with. Oh, for days twice as long! Yet these approach the longest days of the year.

22d. Another glorious day of heat; the sun fairly drove me into the shade to work among the house plants on the piazza. Hot, hot, and bright, and outside the garden growing things begin to pine for showers. When the sun declined toward the west in the afternoon, I sat in the shade and from the veranda turned the hose with its fine sprinkler all over the garden. Oh, the joy of it! The delicious scents from earth and leaves, the glitter of drops on the young green, the gratitude of all the plants at the refreshing bath and draught of water! The rich red Wallflowers sent up fresh clouds of incense, the brilliant and delicate Iceland Poppies bowed their lovely heads and swayed with pleasure at the bright shower. But rain is greatly needed, searching rain which shall drench the ground and reach the roots, and give new life to everything.

23d. Again hot, still, and splendid. Spent all the morning hammering stakes down into the beds near Hollyhocks, Sunflowers, Larkspurs, Lilies, Roses, single Dahlias, and all the tall growing things. Many were tall enough to fasten to the stakes, — all will be, presently. One enormous red Hollyhock grew thirteen feet high by actual measurement before it stopped last year, in a corner near the piazza. Oh, but he was superb! At night the lights from one window streamed through a leafy arch of clambering vine, and illumined him as he swayed to and fro in the wind, a stately column of beauty and grace. A black-red

Hollyhocks in Late Summer

Celia Thaxter's parlor. Photo Isles of Shoals Collection, UNH Media Services. Courtesy of the Star Island Corporation.

comrade leaned against him and mingled its rich blossoms with his brighter color, and near him were rose, pink, and cherry, and white spikes of bloom, lovely to behold. All the afternoon weeding and thinning out the plants. The large bank sloping to the southwest outside the garden is a perfect mass of flowers to be,—no weeds, for I have conquered them; but it is next to impossible to pull up plants enough to give all room. Again and again I have thinned them; now I think I must leave them to their fate and let it be a case of survival of the fittest.

24th. Last night, after having given myself the pleasure of watering the garden, I could not sleep for anxiety about the slugs. I seldom water the flowers at night because the moisture calls them out, and they have an orgy feasting on my most precious children all night long. Before going to bed I went all over the inclosure and, alas, I found them swarming on the Sweet Peas; baby slugs, tiny creatures covering the tender leaves and the dry pea-sticks even, thick as grains of sand. I was in despair, and though I knew they did not mind ashes, I took the fine sifter and covered Peas, sticks, slugs, and all with a thick, smothering cloud of wood ashes. Then I left them with many misgivings and went to bed, but not to sleep, for thinking of them. At twelve o'clock I said to myself, You know the slugs don't care a rap for all the ashes in the world, but the friendly toads may be kept away by them, and who knows if such a smother of them may not

kill the precious Peas themselves ? I could not
bear it any longer, rose up and donned my dress-
ing gown, and out into the dark and dew I bore
the hose, over my shoulders coiled, to the very
farthest corners of the garden, and washed off
every atom of ashes in the black midnight, and
came back and slept in peace.

These are most anxious times on account of
the slugs. Now, every morning when I rise I
go at once into the garden at four o'clock and
make a business of slaughtering them till half
past five, when I stop for breakfast. If the
day is pleasant they are all hidden by that time,
for they dread so the touch of the sun. But in
the hoary morning dew they delight. This is the
hardest part of my gardening, and I rejoice that
not one person in a thousand has this plague of
slugs to fight. It is so difficult to destroy them ;
to see their countless legions and feel so helpless
before their numbers, to find one's most precious
favorites nibbled and ragged, and everything
threatened with destruction is a trial indeed. I
carry a large pepper-box filled with air-slaked lime
and shake it over them everywhere. They are so
small this year that it destroys them ; they turn
milky and miserably perish, but the next morning there are just as many more to take their
places. Still I patiently persevere, carefully
washing off the lime, so anxious lest it should
harm the plants, and killing by hand all the larger
monsters.

In that most charming old book, Gilbert
White's " Natural History of Selborne," I find he

In the Garden

From the Doorway

Home of the Humming-bird

Sunset and the Pinafore

A Shady Seat

The Garden in its Glory

Larkspurs and Lilies

Hollyhocks in Late Summer

The Bride

Poppy Bank in the Early Morning

The Altar and Shrine

A Favorite Corner

speaks of these arch enemies of mine as " un-
noticed myriads of small shell-less snails called
slugs, which silently and imperceptibly make
amazing havoc in field and garden ; " adding in a
note, " Farmer Young of Norton Farm says that
this spring (1777) about four acres of his wheat
in one field were entirely destroyed by the slugs,
which swarmed on the blades of corn and devoured
it as fast as it sprung."

Poor Farmer Young! I deeply sympathize
with him and his long buried trouble!

Again White says : " The shell-less snails called
slugs are in motion all winter in mild weather and
commit great depredations on garden plants, and
much injure the green wheat."

There was a happy time when such a thing as
a slug was unknown on my island, and I well remember the first that were brought here among
some Moonflowers that were imported from a distant green-house. I saw them adhering to the
outside of the flower-pots and did not kill them,
never dreaming what powers of evil they would
become!

25th. Every day the garden grows more interesting, more fascinating. Buds full of promise
show themselves on the single Dahlias whose
seeds were only planted in February ; on the Rose
Campions, the perennial kind, on the tall white
Lilies. The Hollyhocks are thick with buds, and
rich spikes head all the boughs of the Larkspurs,
and as for the Roses, they are simply wonderful.
The Tea Roses are loaded with buds ; on one of
the Polyanthas that lived all winter in the ground

I counted fifty-two, and it is a tiny bush not more than a foot high. The dear old Sweet Rocket is blossoming in every corner, sending up its grateful perfume. Now come days of great anxiety about the Margaret Carnations that I have so loved and watched and tended since the first of March. They were splendid plants, full of health and strength and all ready to bloom. Alas, I saw, a day or two ago, the leaves turning yellow. I knew too well what that meant. There was but one thing to do. Down on my knees I went this morning, and bringing my face close to the ground, began pulling apart the central shoot in each plant, where the sickly color hung its flag of distress for a signal. Down, down a cruel length, into the very heart and core of each precious stem I tore my reluctant way to find that abomination of which I was in search, namely, a short fat lively white worm; for him I probed and brought him up on the point of a pin, and having a small quantity of alcohol at hand for the purpose, dropped him into it forthwith, for instant and complete destruction. Over forty of these beasts did I destroy, and left the tattered Pinks to rest and recover, if they could, poor things, after such a terrible experience! These worms seem made for all fragrant Pinks; as far as my experience goes they never attack anything else. How in the world, I wonder, do they know where the Carnations are planted and when to come for them? Such a scene of devastation as is my pretty bed of Pinks of which I was so proud, dwarfed and yellow, with their gnawed-off leaves strewn about

all over the ground! But they will put out side
shoots and patiently strive to fulfill heaven's intent for them, of which they are conscious from
the least root-tip to the end of every battered leaf.
There is something pathetic as well as wonderful
in the way in which these growing things of almost all kinds meet disaster and discouragement.
Should they suffer misfortune like this, — the lop-
ping of a limb, or the losing of buds, or any sap-
ping of their vitality, — if the cause is removed,
they will try so hard to repair damages, send out
new shoots, make strenuous efforts to recover the
lost ground, and still perfect blossom and fruit as
nature meant they should. There is a lesson to
be learned of them on which I have often pondered.

June 3d. This has been an exciting day, for the
Water Lilies I sent for a week ago came in a mysterious damp box across the ocean foam! I had
made their tubs all ready for them, putting in the
bottom of each the " well-rotted manure," and over
this rich earth and sand mixed in proper propor-
tions. These tubs, or rather large, tall butter firkins,
stood ready in their places along the sunniest and
most sheltered bed in the garden. Oh, the pleasure of opening that box and finding each unfamiliar treasure packed so carefully in wet moss,
each folded in oiled paper to keep it moist, and
each labeled with its fascinating name! The great
pink Lotus of Egypt, the purple Lily of Zanzibar, and the red one of the same sort, the golden
Chromatella, the pure white African variety and
the smaller native white one, the yellow Water

Poppy and the little exquisite plant called Parrot's Feather, that creeps all about over the water and has the wonderful living, metallic green of the plumage of the handsome green parrots. These, with the flourishing Water Hyacinth I already had growing in its tub on the steps, and the bright pink Cape Cod Lily, make ten tubs of water plants, — a most breathlessly interesting family! And I must not forget another tub of seedling Water-Lilies that I am watching with the most intense interest also. It took most of the long, happy day to plant all these in the rich wet mud and settle them in their comfortable quarters. I laid some horseshoes I had picked up at different times, and saved, round the roots to hold them down temporarily, while I gently flooded the tubs with water and rejoiced to see the lovely leaves float out on the surface fresh as if they were at home. Then I sifted clean beach sand over the earth about them, to the depth of an inch or more, to hold the soil down and keep the water clear, and all was done. What delight to look forward to the watching and tending of these new friends! I find myself wondering what enemy will attack these, for surely something has been made for their destruction, which I must fight! There is not a growing thing in the garden that has not its enemies and destroyers, fortunate if it has only one. Just at this time there is a rampant little snuff-colored spider which comes in from the grass and fastens upon tender growths in the bor-ders about the house, covering the succulent leaves and stems of Wild Cucumbers and Morning-glories, and even Nasturtiums and Cornflowers, so thickly that the plant is not to be seen at all for them; they are like a brown glove over every leaf, and they suck every drop of sap out of the plant, leaving it perfectly white. They are fatal on the Sweet Peas, of which they are especially fond. No poison known to me has the slightest effect on them; nothing but water turned on with the hose in floods disturbs them. This washes them away for the time being. It has to be repeated, however, many times a day, for they recover from their drenching and return to their work of devastation with renewed vigor. Fortunately these do not, like the slugs, last forever; they are gone in less than six weeks; but they keep me busy indeed while they stay.

I am obliged to spend a good deal of time just now hunting and destroying different bugs and worms and so forth. The blue-green aphis appears on certain precious Honeysuckle buds, and must be vigorously syringed with fir-tree oil before he gets a foothold and spreads his hideous legions everywhere. Also the lively worm that ties the Rose leaves together and gobbles them up and hides in a web within them, that I may find and crush him; and the white thrip which calls for hellebore, on the under side of them, and many more, must be attended to before they wax strong and bold in their villainy and defy me. A curious plague, if I may call it so, has come upon the little garden, in the shape of the delicious edible mushrooms, Coprinus Comatus, which come up all over the place and with slow strength heave the

ground and my flowers into heaps, thrusting
handsome long ivory-white, umbrella-shaped heads
on stems a foot long, up high above and over
most things in the beds. But these are eaten as
soon as they appear, and are not such a very
great trial, though I would rather they left my
dear flowers undisturbed.

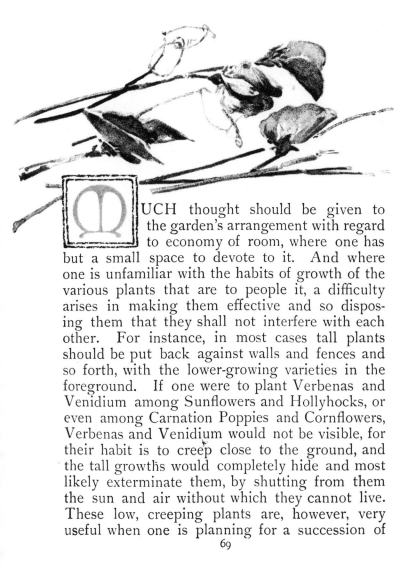

MUCH thought should be given to the garden's arrangement with regard to economy of room, where one has but a small space to devote to it. And where one is unfamiliar with the habits of growth of the various plants that are to people it, a difficulty arises in making them effective and so disposing them that they shall not interfere with each other. For instance, in most cases tall plants should be put back against walls and fences and so forth, with the lower-growing varieties in the foreground. If one were to plant Verbenas and Venidium among Sunflowers and Hollyhocks, or even among Carnation Poppies and Cornflowers, Verbenas and Venidium would not be visible, for their habit is to creep close to the ground, and the tall growths would completely hide and most likely exterminate them, by shutting from them the sun and air without which they cannot live. These low, creeping plants are, however, very useful when one is planning for a succession of flowers. I plant Pansies, Verbenas, Drummond's Phlox, and so forth, among my Pinks and Wall-flowers and others of like compact habit, so that, when the higher slender plants have done blossoming, the others, which seldom cease flowering till frost, may still clothe the ground with color and beauty. Of course it goes without saying that climbing Vines should not be set where there is nothing upon which they may climb. Indeed that would be simple cruelty — nothing more nor less. Everything that needs it should be given a support without fail — all the myriad lovely Vines that one may have with so little trouble, and which seem to have been made to wreathe the dwellings of men with freshness and beauty and grace. The long list of varieties of flowering Clematis, so many shapes and colors, the numerous Honeysuckles, the Wistaria, Passion - flowers, Morning-glories, Hops, the Dutchman's Pipe, the Cobœas, Woodbine, and many others, not counting Sweet Peas and Nasturtiums, — these last among the most beautiful and decorative of all, — every one is twice as valuable if given the support it demands. In the case of Nasturtiums, however, which seem with endless good-nature ready to adapt themselves to any conditions of existence, except, perhaps, being expected to live in a swamp, it is not so important that they should have something upon which to climb. A very good way is to put them near a rock one wishes to have covered, or to let them run down a bank upon which nothing else cares to grow. They will clothe such places with wild and beautiful luxuriance of green leaves and glowing flowers.

It seems strange to write a book about a little garden only fifty feet long by fifteen wide! But then, as a friend pleasantly remarked to me, "it extends upward," and what it lacks in area is more than compensated by the large joy that grows out of it and its uplifting and refreshment of "the Spirit of Man."

I have made a plan of this minute domain to show how it may be possible to accomplish much within such narrow compass, and also to give an idea of an advantageous method of grouping in a space so confined. I have not room to experiment with rockworks and ribbon-borders and the like, nor should I do it even if I had all the room in the world. For mine is just a little old-fashioned garden where the flowers come together to praise the Lord and teach all who look upon them to do likewise.

All through the months of April and May, when the weather is not simply impossible, I am at work in it, and also through most of June. It is wonderful how much work one can find to do in so tiny a plot of ground. But in the latter weeks of June there comes a time when I can begin to take breath and rest a little from these difficult yet pleasant labors; an interval when I may take time to consider, a morning when I may seek the hammock in the shady piazza, and, looking across my happy flower beds, let the sweet day sink deep into my heart. From the flower beds I look over the island slopes to the sea, and realize it all, — the rapture of growth, the delicious shades of green that clothe the ground, Wild

Rose, Bayberry, Spirea, Shadbush, Elder, and many more. How beautiful they are, these grassy, rocky slopes shelving gradually to the sea, with here and there a mass of tall, blossoming grass softly swaying in the warm wind against the peaceful, pale blue water! Among the grass a few ghostly dandelion tops yet linger, with now and then a belated golden flower. How lovely is the delicacy of the white bleached rocks, the little spaces of shallow soil exquisite with vivid crimson Sorrel, or pearly with the brave Eyebright, all against the soft color of the sea. What harmony of movement in all these radiant growths just stirred by the gentle air! Here and there a stout little bough of Chokecherry, with clustered white blossoms tipped with pink, springing from a cleft in the rock, lights up in sunshine, its pink more glowing for the turquoise background of the ocean. How hot the sun blazes! The Blue-eyed Grass is quite faint and drooping in the rich turf, but the yellow Crowfoot shines strong and steady; no sunshine is too bright for it. In the garden the tall Jacqueminot Rosebushes gather power from the great warmth and light, and hold out their thick buds to absorb it and fold its splendor in their inmost hearts. One or two of the heaviest buds begin to loosen their crimson velvet petals and shed their delicious perfume on the air. The Oriental Poppy glories in the heat. Among its buds, thrust upward like solid green apples, one has burst into burning flame, each of its broad fiery petals as large as the whole inside of my hand. In the Iceland Poppy bed the ardent light

PLAN OF GARDEN WITH LIST OF FLOWERS

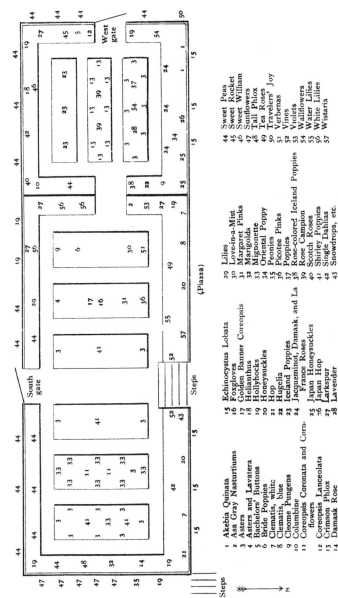

1 Akebia Quinata
2 Asa Gray Nasturtiums
3 Asters
4 Asters and Lavatera
5 Bachelors' Buttons
6 Bride Poppies
7 Clematis, white
8 Clematis, blue
9 Cleome Pungens
10 Columbine
11 Coreopsis Coronata and Cornflowers
12 Coreopsis Lanceolata
13 Crimson Phlox
14 Damask Rose
15 Echinocystus Lobata
16 Foxgloves
17 Golden Banner Coreopsis
18 Helianthus
19 Hollyhocks
20 Honeysuckles
21 Hop
22 Hugelia
23 Iceland Poppies
24 Jacqueminot, Damask, and La France Roses
25 Japan Honeysuckles
26 Japan Hop
27 Larkspur
28 Lavender

29 Lilies
30 Love-in-a-Mist
31 Margaret Pinks
32 Marigolds
33 Mignonette
34 Oriental Poppy
35 Peonies
36 Picotee Pinks
37 Poppies
38 Rose-colored Iceland Poppies
39 Rose Campion
40 Scotch Roses
41 Shirley Poppies
42 Single Dahlias
43 Snowdrops, etc.

44 Sweet Peas
45 Sweet Rocket
46 Sweet William
47 Sunflowers
48 Tall Phlox
49 Tea Roses
50 Travelers' Joy
51 Verbenas
52 Vines
53 Violets
54 Wallflowers
55 Water Lilies
56 White Lilies
57 Wistaria

NOTE.—The garden is 50 ft. long by 15 ft. wide, and is surrounded by a border of all sorts of mixed flowers. A bank of flowers at the southwest corner slopes from the garden fence.

has wooed a graceful company of drooping buds
to blow, and their cups of delicate fire, orange and
yellow, sway lightly on stems as slender as grass.
In sheltered corners the Forget-me-not spreads its
cool, heaven-blue clusters; by the fence "the Larkspurs listen" while they wait; the large purple
Pansies shrink and turn from the too brilliant gaze
of the sun. Rose Campions, Tea Roses, Mignonette, Marigolds, Coreopsis, the rows of Sweet Peas,
the broad-leaved Hollyhocks and the rest, rejoice
and grow visibly with every moment of the glorious day. Clematis and Honeysuckle almost seem
to hurry, Nasturtiums reach their shield-like leaves
and wind the stems thereof round any and every
stick and string they can touch by which to lift
themselves, here and there showing their first
glowing flowers, and climbing eagerly. The long
large buds of the white Clematis, the earliest of
all, are swelling visibly before my eyes, and the
buds of the early June Honeysuckle are reddening
at the end of every spray. In one corner a tall
purple Columbine hangs its myriad clustered
bells; each flower has six shell-like whorls set in a
circle, colored like rich amethysts and lined with
lustrous silver, white as frost. Cornflowers like
living sparks of exquisite color, rose and azure,
white and purple, twinkle all over the place, and
the heavenly procession begins in good earnest.
The Grapevine smooths out its young leaves, —
they are woolly and crimson; the wind blows and
shows me their grayish-white under surfaces. I
think of Browning's tender song, the verse, —

" The leaf buds on the vine are woolly,
I noticed that to-day,
One day more bursts them open fully,
You know the red turns gray."

The Echinocystus plants that have sprung in
thick ranks along the edge of the beds against
the piazza are fairly storming up the trellis, having sown themselves in the autumn; they have
just really begun to take firm hold, and are climbing hand over hand, as sailors do, with their strong
green tendrils stretching out like arms and hands
to right and left, laying hold of every available
thing by which to cling and spring upward to the
very eaves. There in August they form a closely
woven curtain of lush, light green, overhung with
large, loose clusters of starry white flowers having
a pure, delicious fragrance like honey and the
wax of the comb.

Now come the most perfect days of the year,
blue days, hot on the continent, but heavenly here,
where the cool breeze breathes round the islands
from the great expanse of whispering water. Delightful it is to lie here and rest and realize all
this beauty and rejoice in all its joy! The distant coast-line is dim in soft mirage.

" Half lost in the liquid azure bloom of a crescent of sea,
The silent, sapphire-spangled, marriage-ring of the land."

It lies so lovely, far away! At its edge the
water is glassy calm, the houses and large, glimmering piles of buildings along its whole length
show white in the hot haze; in the offing the far-
off sails are half lost in this shimmering veil;

The Bride

The Appledore House photographed from Celia's garden.

farther out there is a soft wind blowing; little
fishing-boats with their sails furled lie at anchor
between us and the land, faintly outlined against
the delicate tone of the water. All is so still! I
hear a bee go blundering into the Bachelor's Buttons that hold up their flowers to the sun like
small, compact yellow Roses. Suddenly comes a
gush of the song-sparrow's music, but father martin sits at his door very quiet; it is too hot on the
red roof of his little house, so he sits at its portal
and meditates while his small wife broods within,
only now and then from his pretty throat pours a
low ripple of sound, melodiously content. I am
conscious of the sandpiper calling and the full tide
murmuring, and I, too, am content.

Outside the garden fence it is as if the flowers
had broken their bounds and were rushing down
the sloping bank in a torrent of yellow, where the
early Artemisias and Eschscholtzias are hastening
into bloom, overflowing in a flood of gold that,
lightly stirred by every breeze, sends a satin shim-
mer to the sun. Eschscholtzia — it is an ugly name
for a most lovely flower. California Poppy is
much better. Down into the sweet plot I go and
gather a few of these, bringing them to my little
table and sitting down before them the better to
admire and adore their beauty. In the slender
green glass in which I put them they stand
clothed in their delicate splendor. One blossom
I take in a loving hand the more closely to examine
it, and it breathes a glory of color into sense and
spirit which is enough to kindle the dullest imagi-
nation. The stems and fine thread-like leaves are

smooth and cool gray-green, as if to temper the
fire of the blossoms, which are smooth also, un-
like almost all other Poppies, that are crumpled
past endurance in their close green buds, and
make one feel as if they could not wait to break
out of the calyx and loosen their petals to the
sun, to be soothed into even tranquillity of beauty
by the touches of the air.   Every cool gray-green
leaf is tipped with a tiny line of red, every flower-
bud wears a little pale-green pointed cap like an
elf, and in the early morning, when the bud is
ready to blow, it pushes off the pretty cap and unfolds all its loveliness to the sun.   Nothing could
be more picturesque than this fairy cap, and nothing more charming than to watch the blossom
push it off and spread its yellow petals, slowly
rounding to the perfect cup.   As I hold the flower
in my hand and think of trying to describe it, I
realize how poor a creature I am, how impotent
are words in the presence of such perfection.   It
is held upright upon a straight and polished
stem, its petals curving upward and outward into
the cup of light, pure gold with a lustrous satin
sheen; a rich orange is painted on the gold, drawn
in infinitely fine lines to a point in the centre of
the edge of each petal, so that the effect is that
of a diamond of flame in a cup of gold.   It is not
enough that the powdery anthers are orange bordered with gold; they are whirled about the very
heart of the flower like a revolving Catherine-
wheel of fire.   In the centre of the anthers is a
shining point of warm sea-green, a last, consummate touch which makes the beauty of the blos-

som supreme. Another has the orange suffused
through the gold evenly, almost to the outer
edges of the petals, which are left in bright, light
yellow with a dazzling effect. Turning the flower
and looking at it from the outside, it has no calyx,
but the petals spring from a simple pale-green
disk, which must needs be edged with sea-shell
pink for the glory of God! The fresh splendor
of this flower no tongue nor pen nor brush of
mortal man can fitly represent.

Who indeed shall adequately describe any one,
the simplest even, of these radiant beings? Day
after day, as I watch them appear, one variety
after another, in such endless changes of delicate
beauty, I can but marvel ever more and more at
the exhaustless power of the great Inventor.
Must He not enjoy the work of His hands, the
manifold perfection of these His matchless crea-
tions? Who can behold the unfolding of each
new spring and all its blossoms without feeling
the renewal of " God's ancient rapture," of which
Browning speaks in " Paracelsus "? In that im-
mortal rapture, I, another of his creatures, less
obedient in fulfilling His laws of beauty than are
these lovely beings, do humbly share, reflecting it
with all the powers of my spirit and rejoicing in
His work with an exceeding joy.

As the days go on toward July, the earth becomes dry and all the flowers begin to thirst for
moisture. Then from the hillside, some warm,
still evening, the sweet rain-song of the robin
echoes clear, and next day we wake to a dim
morning; soft flecks of cloud bar the sun's way,

fleecy vapors steal across the sky, the southwest wind blows lightly, rippling the water into little waves that murmur melodiously as they kiss the shore. In this warm gray, brooding light I am reminded of Tennyson's subtle description of such a daybreak: —

"When the first low matin chirp hath grown
Full quire, and morning driven her plough of pearl
Far furrowing into light the mounded rack,
Beyond the fair green field and eastern sea."

Through the early hours of the day the mottled, pearly clouds keep their shape, with delicious open spaces of tempered blue between; by and by the sky's tender fleece is half shadowed, toward noon it melts into loose mists. Color everywhere tells against these pellucid grays, — the gold of Lemon Lilies, the flame of Iceland Poppies, all the sweet tints of every blossom. Presently the happy rain begins to fall, so soft, so warm, so peaceful, the very sound of it is a pleasure; every leaf in the patient garden, which has waited for the shower so long, spreads itself wide to catch each crystal drop and treasure its deep refreshment. All day it rains; at night the melody lulls us to sleep as it patters on the roof. In the night the wind changes, and next day brings a northeast storm again with a wild wind, but from this the little flower plot is well protected, and I rejoice in the thorough watering deep down among their roots which is doing all the plants unmeasured good. Two, perhaps three days, it lasts, the gale blowing till there is such contention of winds and waves about the little isle as to make a ceaseless

roaring of wild breakers round its shores. When
at last the tempest wears itself out, what delight
there is in the great tranquillity that follows it,
what music in the soft, far murmurs of ceasing
strife in air and ocean, spent wrath that seems to
breathe yet in an undertone, half sullen, half re-
lenting, while the broad yellow light that lies over
sea and rocks in stillness, like a quiet smile,
promises a heavenly day on the morrow.

Then, with what fresh wealth of color and perfume the garden will meet the resplendent sunrise! Every moment it grows more and more
beautiful. I think for wondrous variety, for certain picturesque qualities, for color and form
and a subtle mystery of character, Poppies seem,
on the whole, the most satisfactory flowers among
the annuals. There is absolutely no limit to their
variety of color. They are the tenderest lilac, the
deepest crimson, richest scarlet, white with softest
suffusion of rose; all shades of rose, clear light
pink with sea-green centre, the anthers in a golden
halo about it; black and fire-color; red that is
deepened to black, with gray reflections; cherry-
color, with a cross of creamy white at the bottom
of the cup, and round its central altar of ineffable
golden green again the halo of yellow anthers;
purple, with rich splashes of a deeper shade of the
same color, with grayish white rays about the
centre; all shades of lavender and lilac; exquisite smoke-color, in some cases delicately touched
and freaked with red; some pure light gray,
some of these gray ones edged with crimson or
scarlet; there are all tints of mauve. To tell all

the combinations of their wonderful hues, or even
half, would be quite impossible, from the simple
transparent scarlet bell of the wild Poppy to the
marvelous pure white, the wonder of which no
tongue can tell. Oh, these white Poppies, some
with petals more delicate than the finest tissue
paper, with centres of bright gold, some of thicker
quality, large, shell-like petals, almost ribbed in
their effect, their green knob in the middle like a
boss upon a shield, rayed about with beautiful
grayish yellow stamens, as in the kind called the
Bride. Others — they call this kind the Snowdrift
— have thick double flowers, deeply cut and fringed
at the edges, the most opaque white, and full of
exquisite shadows. Then there are the Iceland-
ers, which Lieutenant Peary found making gay
the frosty fields of Greenland, in buttercup-yel-
low and orange and white; the great Orientals,
gorgeous beyond expression; the immense single
white California variety. I could not begin to
name them all in the longest summer's day! The
Thorn Poppy, Argemone, is a fascinating variety,
most quaint in method of growth and most decorative. As for the Shirleys, they are children
of the dawn, and inherit all its delicate, vivid,
delicious suffusions of rose-color in every conceivable shade. Of the Poppy one of the great
masters of English prose discourses in this wise.
Speaking of the common wild Poppy of the English fields, which grows broadcast also over most
of Europe, he says: " The splendor of it is proud,
almost insolently so," which immediately brings to
mind Browning's lines in " Sordello," —

Poppy Bank in the Early Morning

Celia Thaxter and friends gathered on her piazza. From left are: Mrs. Hepworth, author Amy L. Stoddard, Mrs. Charlotte Dana, Mrs. Childe Hassam, Mary G. Stoddard, Celia Thaxter, Childe Hassam. Karl Thaxter photograph.

" The Poppy's red effrontery,
Till autumn spoils its fleering quite with rain,
And portionless, a dry, brown, rattling crane
Protrudes."

Papaver Rhœas is the common wild scarlet Poppy
that both these writers describe. John Ruskin
says : " I have in my hand a small red Poppy
which I gathered on Whit Sunday in the palace
of the Cæsars. It is an intensely simple, intensely floral flower. All silk and flame, a scarlet
cup, perfect edged all round, seen among the wild
grass far away like a burning coal fallen from
Heaven's altars. You cannot have a more complete, a more stainless type of flower absolute ; inside and outside, all flower. No sparing of color
anywhere, no outside coarsenesses, no interior
secrecies, open as the sunshine that creates it ;
fine finished on both sides, down to the extremest
point of insertion on its narrow stalk, and robed
in the purple of the Cæsars. . . .
" Literally so. That Poppy scarlet, so far as
could be painted by mortal hand, for mortal king,
stays yet, against the sun and wind and rain, on
the walls of the house of Augustus, a hundred
yards from the spot where I gathered the weed
of its desolation. . . . The flower in my hand is
a poverty *stricken* Poppy, I was going to write,
poverty *strengthened* Poppy, I mean. On richer
ground it would have gushed into flaunting
breadth of untenable purple ; flapped its incon-
sistent scarlet vaguely to the wind ; dropped the
pride of its petals over my hand in an hour after I
gathered it. But this little rough-bred thing . . .

is as bright and strong to-day as yesterday. . . .
What outline its petals really have is little shown
in their crumpled fluttering, but that very crum-
pling arises from a fine floral character which
we do not enough value in them. We usually
think of a Poppy as a coarse flower; but it is the
most transparent and delicate of all the blossoms
of the field. The rest, nearly all of them, depend on the texture of their surfaces for color.
But the Poppy is painted glass; it never glows
so brightly as when the sun shines through it.
Wherever it is seen, against the light or with the
light, always it is a flame, and warms the wind
like a blown ruby. . . . Gather a green Poppy
bud, just when it shows the scarlet line at its side,
break it open and unpack the Poppy. The whole
flower is there complete in size and color, its
stamens full grown, but all packed so closely that
the fine silk of the petals is crushed into a million
of wrinkles. When the flower opens, it seems a
relief from torture; the two imprisoning green
leaves are shaken to the ground, the aggrieved
corolla smooths itself in the sun and comforts itself as best it can, but remains crushed and hurt
to the end of its days."

I know of no flower that has so many charming tricks and manners, none with a method of
growth more picturesque and fascinating. The
stalks often take a curve, a twist from some current of air or some impediment, and the fine
stems will turn and bend in all sorts of graceful
ways, but the bud is always held erect when the
time comes for it to blossom. Ruskin quotes

Lindley's definition of what constitutes a Poppy, which he thinks "might stand." This is it: "A Poppy is a flower which has either four or six petals, and two or more treasuries united in one, containing a milky, stupefying fluid in its stalks and leaves, and always throwing away its calyx when it blossoms."

I muse over their seed-pods, those supremely graceful urns that are wrought with such matchless elegance of shape, and think what strange power they hold within. Sleep is there, and Death his brother, imprisoned in those mystic sealed cups. There is a hint of their mystery in their shape of sombre beauty, but never a suggestion in the fluttering blossom; it is the gayest flower that blows. In the more delicate varieties the stalks are so slender, yet so strong, like fine grass stems, when you examine them you wonder how they hold even the light weight of the flower so firmly and proudly erect. They are clothed with the finest of fine hairs up and down the stalks, and over the green calyx, especially in the Iceland varieties, where these hairs are of a lovely red-brown color and add much to their beauty.

It is plain to see, as one gazes over the Poppy beds on some sweet evening at sunset, what buds will bloom in the joy of next morning's first sunbeams, for these will be lifting themselves heavenward, slowly and silently, but surely. To stand by the beds at sunrise and see the flowers awake is a heavenly delight. As the first long, low rays of the sun strike the buds, you know they feel the signal! A light air stirs among them; you lift your eyes, perhaps to look at a rosy cloud or follow the flight of a caroling bird, and when you look back again, lo! the calyx has fallen from the largest bud and lies on the ground, two half transparent, light green shells, leaving the flower petals wrinkled in a thousand folds, just released from their close pressure. A moment more and they are unclosing before your eyes. They flutter out on the gentle breeze like silken banners to the sun, and such a color! The orange of the Iceland Poppy is the most ineffable color; it "warms the wind" indeed! I know no tint like it; it is orange dashed with carmine, most like the reddest coals of an intensely burning fire. Look at this exquisite cup: the wind has blown nearly smooth the crinkled petals; these, where they meet in the centre, melt into a delicate greenish yellow. In the heart of the blossom rises a round green altar, its sides penciled with nine black lines, and a nine-rayed star of yellow velvet clasps the flat, pure green top. From the base of this altar springs the wreath of stamens and anthers; the inner circle of these is generally white, the outer yellow, and all held high and clear within the cup. The radiant effect of this arrangement against the living red cannot be told.

The Californias put out their clean, polished, pointed buds straight up to the sun from the first, but all the others have this fashion of drooping theirs till the evening before they blow. There is a kind of triumph in the way they do this, lifting their treasured splendor yet safe within its clasping calyx to be ready to meet the first beams of the day.

The Orientals are glorious, even in the victorious family of Poppies. Ruskin has a chapter on " The Rending of Leaves." I always think of it when I see the large, hairy, rich green leaves of this variety, which are deeply " rent," almost the whole width of the leaf to the midrib. These leaves grow somewhat after the fashion of a Dandelion, spreading several feet in all directions from the centre, which sends up in June immense flower-stalks crowned with heavy apple-like buds, that elongate as they increase in size, till some morning the thick calyx breaks and falls, and the great scarlet flags of the flower unfold. There is a kind of angry brilliance about it, a sombre and startling magnificence. Its large petals are splashed near the base with broad, irregular spots of black-purple, as if they had been struck with a brush full of color. The seed-pod, rising fully an inch high in the centre, is of a luminous, indescribable shade of green, and folded over its top, a third of its height, is a cap of rich lavender, laid down in points evenly about the crown. On the centre of this is a little knob of deep purple velvet, from which eleven rays of the same color curve over the top and into each point of the lavender cap. And round this wonderful seed-pod, with its wealth of elaborate ornament, is a thick girdle of stamens half an inch deep, with row upon row and circle within circle of anthers covered with dust of splendid dusky purple, and held each upon a slender thread of deeper purple still. It is simply superb, and when the great bush is ablaze with these flowers it is indeed a conflagration of color. " The fire-engines always turn out when my Orientals blaze up on the hillside," writes a flower-loving friend to me. No garden should be without these, for they flourish with the least care, are perfectly hardy, and never fail to blossom generously.

HAT every plant should select only its own colors and forms from the great laboratory of Nature has always seemed to me a very wonderful thing. Each plant takes from its surroundings just those qualities which will produce its own especial characteristics and no others, never hesitating and never making a mistake. For instance, the California Poppies, if left to themselves, will take yellow of many resplendent shades for their color, and never vary their cool, gray-green, red-tipped foliage; the Peacock Poppy will be always scarlet-crimson, with a black spot rimmed with white in every petal; the Corn Poppy will be always clear scarlet; the Bride a miracle of lustrous white, and so on. Runge, a noted chemist, says: "A plant is a great chemist: it distinguishes and separates substances more definitely and accurately than man can, with all his skill, his intelligence, and his appliances. . . . The little Daisy, which has painted its 'wee crimson-tipped flowers,' puts the chemist and scientific man to shame, for it has produced its leaf and stem and flowers, and has dyed these with their bright colors from materials which he can never change with all his arts."

By what power do they know how to select each its own hue and shape, when earth and air hold all the tints and forms that the Creator has invented? The subtle knowledge of plants, instinct perhaps would be a better word, is astonishing. If you dig a hole in the ground and put into it a Rosebush, filling one side of the hole with rich earth and the other with poor soil, every root of that Rosebush will leave the poor half to inhabit the rich and nourishing portion. That is a matter of course, but the instinct of the Rose is something to think about, nevertheless.

Some one has said, speaking of a tree, " What an immense amount of vitally organized material has been here gathered together! It is God's own architecture! This mass of vegetable matter is only earth and air that have undergone transmutation. The material alike of wandering zephyrs and rushing storms, of gently descending night-dews and angry thunder-showers has been *here, on this spot*, metamorphosed."

And I should add that into this piece of architecture God has breathed a vital spark, almost a mind, so remarkable is the intelligent action often manifested in many plants and trees.

A famous Frenchman, Camille Flammarion, says: " I know a maple-tree which was dying on the ruins of an old wall, a few feet from good rich

earth (the soil in a ditch), and which in despair
threw out a venturesome root, reached the cov-
eted earth, buried itself there, and gained a solid
footing, so that by degrees, although a motionless
thing, it changed its place, let its original roots
die, and lived resuscitated upon the organ that
had set it free. I have known elms which were
going to eat up the soil of a fertile field, whose
food had been cut off from them by a wide ditch,
and who, therefore, determined to make their
uncut roots pass under the ditch. They suc-
ceeded, and returned to their regular food, much
to the cultivator's astonishment. I know an
heroic Jasmine which went eight times through a
board which kept the light away from it, and
which a teasing observer would put back in the
shade, hoping so to wear out the flower's energy,
but he did not succeed."

This happened in France, but here in New
England I myself know of a great Wistaria
which grew over one side of a fine old house in
an enchanting garden, and which did something
quite as wonderful. It was a triumph of a vine!
The butt or stump, where it emerged from the
ground, was a foot in diameter, and its branches
covered one side of the house, a space of thirty
feet by thirty feet. So large a vine required a
great deal of water, so it sent its roots down eight
feet under the foundation of the house, passed
along under the brick floor of the dairy, a distance
of fifteen feet, making a solid mat of roots under
the whole floor, reached the well and went straight
through the cracks and crevices of its stone wall
to the desired moisture. An elm root in the same

garden went sixty feet or more under the foundation of the house to that same well.

To quote another writer who has carefully observed these things: "Plants have to the full extent of their necessities a power of observation, of discrimination in the selection of their food, a knowledge of where it is to be found, and the power to a considerable extent to obtain it. For instance, if some animal's remains are buried in the garden, say twenty feet from the grapevine, the vine will know it, and the underground part of the vine will at once change its course and make a direct march for this new storehouse of food, and upon reaching it will throw out an incredible number of roots for its consumption. . . . A weeping willow was planted in a dry, gravelly soil on the south side of a house, a situation in every respect unsuited to this tree, which delights in a heavy moist soil; the result was a slow, stunted growth. After a few years in which it barely lived, it surprised its owner by a vigorous growth which was as astonishing as pleasing, and the cause was looked for. It was found the roots in search of food had traveled under the house a distance of some thirty feet to the well, where they took a downward course till they reached the water that furnished the moisture which is essential to the growth of this tree.

"The movements of the squash vine when pressed by hunger or thirst are truly wonderful. During a severe drought if you place a basin of water at night, say two feet to the left or the right of a strong vine, in the morning it will be found bathing in the basin! Is not this an indication of thought in the vine? Does it not indicate a knowledge in the vine analogous to human understanding? . . . There must be some agent employed to bring the vine to the fountain. . . .

"The more we study plant life the more we become convinced that life is a unit, varying in form only, not in principle. Everything capable of reproduction, growth, and development is governed by the same law, and each is but a part of the unit we term life."

Again to quote the famous Frenchman: "When I breathe the perfume of a Rose," he says, "when I admire the beauty of form, the grace of this flower in its freshly opening bloom, what strikes me most is the work of that hidden, unknown, mysterious force which rules over the plant's life and can direct it in the maintenance of its existence, which chooses the proper molecules of air, water, and earth for its nourishment, and which knows, above all, how to assimilate these molecules and group them so delicately as to form this graceful stem, these dainty green leaves, these soft pink petals, these exquisite tints and delicious fragrance. . . .

"This mysterious force is the animating principle of the plant. Put a Lily seed, an acorn, a grain of wheat, and a peach-stone side by side in the ground, each germ will build up its own organism and no other. . . .

"A plant breathes, drinks, eats, selects, refuses, seeks, works, lives, acts, according to its instincts. One does like a charm, another pines, a third is nervous and agitated. The Sensitive Plant shivers and droops its leaves at the slightest touch."

Climbing plants show often a surprising degree of intelligence, reaching out for support as if they had eyes to see. I have known a vine whose head was aimlessly waving in the wind, with nothing near it to which it might cling, turn deliberately round in an opposite direction to that in which it had been growing and seize a line I had stretched for it to grasp, without any help outside itself, and within the space of an hour's time. By manifold ways they cling and climb, many by winding their stems round and round strings or sticks or wires, or whatever is given them, as do the Morning-glories, Hop, Honeysuckle, Wistarias, and many others; but Sweet Peas, Cobœa, and so forth, put out a delicate tendril at the end of each leaf, or rather group of leaves. Nasturtiums, Clematis, and others take a turn with their leaf-stems round anything that comes in their way, and so lift and hold themselves securely, and the Echinocystus or Wild Cucumber has a system of tendrils strong as iron and elastic as India-rubber. It is most interesting to observe them all and ponder on their different charming ways and habits, to help them if they need it, and to sympathize with all their experiences. As I work among my flowers, I find myself talking to them, reasoning and remonstrating with them, and adoring them as if they were human beings. Much laughter I provoke among my friends by so doing, but that is of no consequence. We are on such good terms, my flowers and I !

Altogether lovely they are out of doors, but
I plant and tend them always with the thought
of the joy they will be within the house also. I
know well what Emerson means when he asks,

" Hast thou named all the birds without a gun ?
Loved the wood Rose and left it on its stalk ? "

and if I gather this or any other wild-flower I do
it with such reverent love that even he would be
satisfied. No one knows better and deplores
more deeply than I the wholesale destruction,
wanton and cruel, which goes on among our wildflowers every year; but to bring a few indoors for
purposes of study and fuller appreciation is another and a desirable thing. For the wild Rose
is but partially learned when one pauses a moment in passing to admire the sweet surprise of
its beauty as it suddenly smiles up from the road-
side. It cannot be learned in a single glance,
nor, indeed, in many glances : it must be carefully
considered and lovingly meditated upon before
it yields all the marvel of its delicate glory to
your intelligence. " Consider the Lilies," said the
Master. Truly, there is no more prayerful business than this " consideration " of all the flowers
that grow.

And in the garden they are planted especially
to feast the souls that hunger for beauty, and
within doors as well as without they " delight the
spirit of man." Opening out on the long piazza
over the flower beds, and extending almost its
whole length, runs the large, light, airy room
where a group of happy people gather to pass the

swiftly flying summers here at the Isles of Shoals.
This room is made first for music; on the polished
floor is no carpet to muffle sound, only a few rugs
here and there, like patches of warm green moss
on the pine-needle color given by the polish to
the natural hue of the wood. There are no heavy
draperies to muffle the windows, nothing to absorb the sound. The piano stands midway at
one side; there are couches, sofas with pillows
of many shades of dull, rich color, but mostly of
warm shades of green. There are low bookcases
round the walls, the books screened by short cur-
tains of pleasant olive-green; the high walls to
the ceiling are covered with pictures, and flowers
are everywhere. The shelves of the tall mantel
are splendid with massed Nasturtiums like a blazing torch, beginning with the palest yellow, almost
white, and piled through every deepening shade
of gold, orange, scarlet, crimson, to the blackest
red; all along the tops of the low bookcases burn
the fires of Marigolds, Coreopsis, large flowers of
the velvet single Dahlias in yellow, flame, and
scarlet of many shades, masses of pure gold summer Chrysanthemums, and many more, — all here
and there interspersed with blossoming grasses
for a touch of ethereal green. On one low bookcase are Shirley Poppies in a roseate cloud. And
here let me say that the secret of keeping Poppies
in the house two whole days without fading is
this: they must be gathered early, before the dew
has dried, in the morning. I go forth between
five and six o'clock to cut them while yet their
gray-green leaves are hoary with dew, taking a tall

The Altar and Shrine

The Laighton family cemetery on Appledore Island. John M. Kingsbury photo.

slender pitcher or bottle of water with me into the garden, and as I cut each stem dropping the flower at once into it, so that the stem is covered nearly its whole length with water; and so on till the pitcher is full. Gathered in this way, they have no opportunity to lose their freshness, indeed, the exquisite creatures hardly know they have been gathered at all. When I have all I need, I begin on the left end of this bookcase, which most felicitously fronts the light, and into the glasses put the radiant blossoms with an infinite enjoyment of the work. The glasses (thirty-two in all) themselves are beautiful: nearly all are white, clear and pure, with a few pale green and paler rose and delicate blue, one or two of richer pink, all brilliantly clear and filled with absolutely colorless water, through which the stems show their slender green lengths. Into the glasses at this end on the left I put first the dazzling white single Poppy, the Bride, to lead the sweet procession, — a marvelous blossom, whose pure white is half transparent, with its central altar of ineffable green and gold. A few of these first, then a dozen or more of delicate tissue-paper-like blossoms of snow in still another variety (with petals so thin that a bright color behind them shows through their filmy texture); then the double kind called Snowdrift, which being double makes a deeper body of whiteness flecked with softest shadow. Then I begin with the palest rose tints, placing them next, and slightly mingling a few with the last white ones, — a rose tint delicate as the palm of a baby's hand; then the

next, with a faint suffusion of a blush, and go on
to the next shade, still very delicate, not deeper
than the soft hue on the lips of the great whelk
shells in southern seas; then the damask rose
color and all tints of tender pink, then the deeper
tones to clear, rich cherry, and on to glowing
crimson, through a mass of this to burning
maroon.

The flowers are of all heights (the stems of
different lengths), and, though massed, are in
broken and irregular ranks, the tallest standing
a little over two feet high. But there is no crush-
ing or crowding. Each individual has room to
display its full perfection. The color gathers,
softly flushing from the snow white at one end,
through all rose, pink, cherry, and crimson shades,
to the note of darkest red; the long stems of tender green showing through the clear glass, the
radiant tempered gold of each flower illuminating
the whole. Here and there a few leaves, stalks,
and buds (if I can bring my mind to the cutting
of these last) are sparingly interspersed at the
back. The effect of this arrangement is perfectly
beautiful. It is simply indescribable, and I have
seen people stand before it mute with delight. It
is like the rose of dawn.

To the left of this altar of flowers is a little
table, upon which a picture stands and leans
against the wall at the back. In the picture two
Tea Roses long since faded live yet in their exquisite hues, never indeed to die. Before this I
keep always a few of the fairest flowers, and call
this table the shrine. Sometimes it is a spray of

Madonna Lilies in a long white vase of ground glass, or beneath the picture in a jar of yellow glass floats a saffron-tinted Water Lily, the Chromatella, or a tall sapphire glass holds deep blue Larkspurs of the same shade, or in a red Bohemian glass vase are a few carmine Sweet Peas, another harmony of color, or a charming dull red Japanese jar holds a few Nasturtiums that exactly repeat its hues. The lovely combinations and contrasts of flowers and vases are simply endless.

On another small table below the "altar" are pink Water Lilies in pink glasses and white ones in white glasses ; a low basket of amber glass is filled with the pale turquoise of Forget-me-nots, the glass is iridescent and gleams with changing reflections, taking tints from every color near it. Sweet Peas are everywhere about and fill the air with fragrance ; orange and yellow Iceland Poppies are in tall vases of English glass of light green. There is a large, low bowl, celadon-tinted, and decorated with the boughs and fruit of the Olive on the gray-green background. This is filled with magnificent Jacqueminot Roses, so large, so deep in color as to fully merit the word. Sometimes they are mixed with pink Gabrielle de Luizets and old-fashioned Damask Roses, and the bowl is set where the light falls just as it should to give the splendor of the flowers its full effect. In the centre of a round table under one of the chandeliers is a flaring Venice glass as pure as a drop of dew and of a quaintly lovely shape; on the crystal water therein lies a single white Water Lily, fragrant snow and gold. By itself is a low vase shaped like a Magnolia flower, with petals of light yellow deepening in color at the bottom, where its calyx of olive-green leaves clasps the flower. This has looking over its edge a few pale yellow Nasturtiums of the Asa Gray variety, the lightest of all. With these, one or two of a richer yellow (Dunnett's Orange), the flowers repeating the tones of the vase, and with them harmoniously blending. A large pearly shell of the whelk tribe was given me years ago. I did not know what to do with it. I do not like flowers in shells as a rule, and I think the shells are best on the beach where they belong, but I was fond of the giver, so I sought some way of utilizing the gift. In itself it was beautiful, a mass of glimmering rainbows. I bored three holes in its edge and suspended it from one of the severely simple chandeliers with almost invisible wires. I keep it filled with water and in it arrange sometimes clusters of monthly Honeysuckle sparingly; the hues of the flowers and the shell mingle and blend divinely. I get the same effect with Hydrangea flowers, tints and tones all melt together; so also with the most delicate Sweet Peas, white, rose, and lilac; with these I take some lengths of the blossoming Wild Cucumber vine with its light clusters of white flowers, or the white Clematis, the kind called " Traveler's Joy," and weave it lightly about the shell, letting it creep over one side and, running up the wires, entirely conceal them; then it is like a heavenly apparition afloat in mid air. Sometimes the tender mauve and soft rose and delicate blues of the exquisite little

Rose Campion, or Rose of Heaven, with its grassy foliage, swing in this rainbow shell, making another harmony of hues.

Sometimes it is draped with wild Morning-glory vines which are gathered with their buds at evening; their long wiry stems I coil in the water, and arrange the graceful lengths of leaves and buds carefully, letting a few droop over the edge and twine together beneath the shell, and some run up to the chandelier and conceal the wires. The long smooth buds, yellow-white like ivory, deepen to a touch of bright rose at the tips close folded. In the morning all the buds open into fair trumpets of sea-shell pink, turning to every point of the compass, an exquisite sight to see. By changing the water daily these vines last a week, fresh buds maturing and blossoming every morning.

Near my own seat in a sofa corner at one of the south windows stands yet another small table, covered with a snow-white linen cloth embroidered in silk as white and lustrous as silver. On this are gathered every day all the rarest and loveliest flowers as they blossom, that I may touch them, dwell on them, breathe their delightful fragrance and adore them. Here are kept the daintiest and most delicate of the vases which may best set off the flowers' loveliness, — the smallest of the collection, for the table is only large enough to hold a few. There is one slender small tumbler of colorless glass, from the upper edge of which a crimson stain is diffused half way down its crystal length. In this I keep one glowing

crimson Burgundy Rose, or an opening Jacqueminot bud; the effect is as if the color of the
rose ran down and dyed the glass crimson. It
is so beautiful an effect one never wearies of it.
There is a little jar of Venice glass, the kind
which Browning describes in " The Flight of the
Duchess," —

> " With long white threads distinct inside,
> Like the lake-flower's fibrous roots that dangle
> Loose such a length and never tangle."

This is charming with a few rich Pinks of different shades. Another Venice glass is irregu-
larly bottle-shaped, bluish white with cool sea-
green reflections at the bottom, very delicate, like
an aqua-marine. It is lightly sprinkled with gold
dust throughout its whole length; toward the top
the slender neck takes on a soft touch of pink
which meets and mingles with the Bon Silene or
La France Rose I always keep in it. Another
Venice glass still is a wonder of iridescent blues,
lavenders, gray, and gold, all through, with a faint
hint of elusive green. A spray of heaven-blue
Larkspur dashed with rose is delicious in this
slender shape, with its marvelous tints melting
into the blue and pink of the fairy flowers.

A little glass of crystal girdled with gold holds
pale blue Forget-me-nots; sometimes it is rich
with orange and yellow Erysimum flowers. In
a tall Venetian vase of amber a Lilium auratum
is superb. A low jar of opaque rose-pink, lost at
the bottom in milky whiteness, is refreshing with
an old-fashioned Damask Rose matching its color

A Favorite Corner

Celia's Garden, 1979. Peter Randall photo.

exactly. This is also exquisite with one pink
Water Lily. The pink variety of the Rose Campion is enchanting in this low jar. A tall shaft
of ruby glass is radiant with Poppies of every
shade of rose and lightest scarlet, with the silvery
green of a few oats among them. A slender purple glass is fine with different shades of purple
and lilac Sweet Peas, or one or two purple Poppies, or an Aster or two of just its color, but there
is one long gold-speckled Bohemian glass of rich
green which is simply perfect for any flower that
blows, and perfect under any circumstances. A
half dozen Iceland Poppies, white, yellow, orange,
in a little Japanese porcelain bottle, always stand
on this beautiful table, the few flecks of color on
the bottle repeating their tints. I never could
tell half the lovely combinations that glow on this
table all summer long.

By the wide western window a large vase of
clear white glass, nearly three feet high, stands
full of spears of timothy grass taller than the vase,
the tallest I can find, springing stately and high,
their heavy green tops bending the fine strong
stems just enough for consummate grace. These
are mixed with lighter branching grasses, and
down among the grass stalks are thrust the slender stalks of tall Poppies of every conceivable
shade of red; the whole is a great sheaf of splendor reaching higher than the top of the window.
This is really imposing; it takes the eye with delight.

All summer long within this pleasant room the
flowers hold carnival in every possible combina-

tion of beauty. All summer long it is kept fresh
and radiant with their loveliness, — a wonder of
bloom, color, and fragrance. Year after year a
long procession of charming people come and go
within its doors, and the flowers that glow for
their delight seem to listen with them to the music that stirs each blossom upon its stem. Often
have I watched the great red Poppies drop their
fiery petals wavering solemnly to the floor, stricken
with arrows of melodious sound from the matchless violin answering to the touch of a master, or
to the storm of rich vibrations from the piano.
What heavenly music has resounded from those
walls, what mornings and evenings of pleasant-
ness have flown by in that room! How many
people who have been happy there have gone
out of it and of the world forever! Yet still the
summers come, the flowers bloom, are gathered
and adored, not without wistful thought of the
eyes that will see them no more. Still in the
sweet tranquil mornings at the piano one sits
playing, also with a master's touch, and strains of
Schubert, Mozart, Schumann, Chopin, Rubin-
stein, Beethoven, and many others, soothe and
enchant the air. The wild bird's song that breaks
from without into the sonata makes no discord.
Open doors and windows lead out on the vine-
wreathed veranda, with the garden beyond steeped
in sunshine, a sea of exquisite color swaying in
the light air. Poppies blowing scarlet in the
wind, or delicately flushing in softest rose or
clearest red, or shining white where the Bride
stands tall and fair, like a queen among them all.

A thousand varied hues amid the play of fluttering leaves: Marigolds ablaze in vivid flame; purple Pansies, — a myriad flowers, white, pink, blue, carmine, lavender, in waves of sweet color and perfume to the garden fence, where stand the sentinel Sunflowers and Hollyhocks, gorgeously arrayed and bending gently to the breeze; Sunflowers with broad faces that seem to reflect the glory of the day; the Hollyhocks, tall spikes of pale and deep pink, white, scarlet, yellow, maroon, and many hues. Over the sweet sea of flowers the butterflies go wavering on airy wings of white and gold, the bees hum in the Hollyhocks, and the humming-birds glitter like jewels in the sun; but whether these their winged lovers go or come, the flowers do not care, they live their happy lives and rejoice, intent only on fulfilling Heaven's will, to grow and to blossom in the utmost perfection possible to them. Climbing the trellis, the monthly Honeysuckle holds its clusters high against the pure sunlit sky, glowing in beauty beyond any words of mine to tell. Charming people sit within the pleasant room among its flowers, listening to the delicious music; others are grouped without in the sun-flecked shadow of the green vines, where the cool air ripples lightly in the leaves; lovely women in colors that seem to have copied the flowers in the garden, and all steeped in sweet dreams and fugitive fancies as delicate as the perfumes that drift in soft waves from the blossoms below. Beyond the garden the green grassy spaces sloping to the sea are rich with blossoming thickets of wild Roses, among the bleached white ledges, blushing fair to see, and the ocean beyond shimmers and sparkles beneath the touch of the warm south wind.

Enchanting days, and evenings still more so, if that were possible! With the music still thrilling within the lighted room where the flowers glow under the lamplight, while floods of moonlight make more mystic the charmed night without. The thick curtain of the green vine that drapes the piazza is hung over its whole surface with the long drooping clusters of its starry flowers that lose all their sweetness upon the air, and show from the garden beneath like an immense airy veil of delicate white lace in the moonlight, — a wonderful white glory. Through the windows cut in this living curtain of leaves and flowers we look out over the sea beneath the moon — is anything more mysteriously beautiful? — on glimmering waves and shadowy sails and rocks dim in broken light and shade; on the garden with all its flowers so full of color that even in the moonlight their hues are visibly glowing. The fair creatures stand still, unstirred by any wandering airs, the Lilies gleam, and the white stars of the Nicotiana, the white Poppies, the white Asters that just begin to bloom, and the tall milky clusters of the Phlox: nothing disturbs their slumber save perhaps the wheeling of the rosy-winged Sphinx moth that flutters like the spirit of the night above them as they dream.

THE garden suffers from the long drought in this last week of July, though I water it faithfully. The sun burns so hot that the earth dries again in an hour, after the most thorough drenching I can give it. The patient flowers seem to be standing in hot ashes, with the air full of fire above them. The cool breeze from the sea flutters their drooping petals, but does not refresh them in the blazing noon. Outside the garden on the island slopes the baked turf cracks away from the heated ledges of rock, and all the pretty growths of Sorrel and Eyebright, Grasses and Crowfoot, Potentilla and Lion's-tongue, are crisp and dead. All things begin again to pine and suffer for the healing touch of the rain.

Toward noon on this last day of the month the air darkens, and around the circle of the horizon the latent thunder mutters low. Light puffs of wind eddy round the garden, and whirl aloft the weary Poppy petals high in air, till they wheel like birds about the chimney-tops. Then all is quiet once more. In the rich, hot sky the clouds pile themselves slowly, superb white heights of thunder-heads warmed with a brassy glow that deepens to rose in their clefts toward the sun. These clouds grow and grow, showing like Alpine summits amid the shadowy heaps of looser vapor; all the great vault of heaven gathers darkness ; soon the cloudy heights, melting, are suffused in each other, losing shape and form and color. Then over the coast-line the sky turns a hard gray-green, against which rises with solemn movement and awful deliberation an arch of leaden vapor spanning the heavens from southwest to northeast, livid, threatening, its outer edges shaped like the curved rim of a mushroom, gathering swiftness as it rises, while the water beneath is black as hate, and the thunder rolls peal upon peal, as faster and faster the wild arch moves upward into tremendous heights above our heads. The whole sky is dark with threatening purple. Death and destruction seem ready to emerge from beneath that flying arch of which the livid fringes stream like gray flame as the wind rends its fierce and awful edge. Under it afar on the black level water a single sail gleams chalk-white in the gloom, a sail that even as we look is furled away from our sight, that the frail craft which bears it may ride out the gale under bare poles, or drive before it to some haven of safety. Earth seems to hold her breath before the expected fury. Lightning scores the sky from zenith to horizon, and across from north to south "a fierce, vindictive scribble of fire" writes its blinding way, and the awesome silence is broken

by the cracking thunder that follows every flash.
A moment more, and a few drops like bullets
strike us; then the torn arch flies over in tattered rags, a monstrous apparition lost in darkness; then the wind tears the black sea into white
rage and roars and screams and shouts with triumph, — the floods and the hurricane have it all
their own way. Continually the tempest is shot
through with the leaping lightning and crashing
thunder, like steady cannonading, echoing and
reëchoing, roaring through the vast empty spaces
of the heavens. In pauses of the tumult a strange
light is fitful over sea and rocks, then the tempest begins afresh as if it had taken breath and
gained new strength. One's whole heart rises
responding to the glory and the beauty of the
storm, and is grateful for the delicious refreshment of the rain. Every leaf rejoices in the life-
giving drops. Through the dense sparkling rain-
curtain the lightning blazes now in crimson and
in purple sheets of flame. Oh, but the wind is
wild! Spare my treasures, oh, do not slay utterly my beautiful, beloved flowers! The tall
stalks bend and strain, the Larkspurs bow. I
hold my breath while the danger lasts, thinking
only of the wind's power to harm the garden; for
the leaping lightning and the crashing thunder I
love, but the gale fills me with dread for my flowers defenseless. Still down pour the refreshing
floods; everything is drenched: where are the
humming-birds? The boats toss madly on the
moorings, the sea breaks wildly on the shore,
the world is drowned and gone, there is nothing

but tempest and tumult and rush and roar of wind
and rain.

The long trailing sprays of the Echinocystus
vine stretch and strain like pennons flying out in
the blast, the Wistaria tosses its feathery plumes
over the arch above the door. Alas, for my bank
of tall Poppies and blue Cornflowers and yellow
Chrysanthemums outside ! The Poppies are laid
low, never to rise again, but the others will gather
themselves together by and by, and the many-
colored fires of Nasturtiums will clothe the slope
with new beauty presently. The storm is sweep-
ing past, already the rain diminishes, the lightning pales, the thunder retreats till leagues and
leagues away we hear it "moaning and calling
out of other lands." The clouds break away and
show in the west glimpses of pure, melting blue,
the sun bursts forth, paints a rainbow in the east
upon the flying fragments of the storm, and pours
a flood of glory over the drowned earth ; the
pelted flowers take heart and breathe again, every
leaf shines, dripping with moisture; the grassy
slopes laugh in sweet color; the sea calms itself
to vast tranquillity and answers back the touch
of the sun with a million glittering smiles.

Though the outside bank of flowers is wrecked
and the tall Poppies prone upon the ground, those
inside the garden are safe because I took the pre-
caution to run two rows of wire netting up and
down through the beds for their support. So,
when the winds are cruelly violent, the tall, brittle
stalks lean against this light but strong bulwark
and are unhurt.

After the storm, in the clear, beautiful morning, before sunrise I went as usual into the garden to gather my flowers. To and fro, up and down over the ruined bank I passed ; the wind blew cool and keen from the west, though the sky was smiling. The storm had beaten the flowers flat all over the slope; in scarlet and white and blue and pink and purple and orange bloom they were prostrate everywhere, leaves, stalks, blossoms, and all tangled and matted in an inextricable confusion. Swiftly I made my way through it, finding a foothold here and there, and stooping for every freshly unfolded cup or star or bell whose bud the tempest had spared. As I neared the little western gate with my hands full of blossoms to enter the garden on my way to the house, I was stopped still as a statue before a most pathetic sight. There, straight across the way, a tall Poppy plant lay prone upon the ground, and clinging to the stem of one of its green seed-pods sat my precious pet humming-bird, the dearest of the flock that haunt the garden, the tamest of them all. His eyes were tightly closed, his tiny claws clasped the stem automatically, he had no feeling, he was rigid with cold. The chill dew loaded the gray-green Poppy leaves, the keen wind blew sharply over him, — he is dead, I thought with a pang, as I shifted my flowers in a glowing heap to my left arm, and clasped the frozen little body in the palm of my right hand. It was difficult to disengage his slender wiry claws from their close grip on the chilly stalk, but he never moved or showed a sign of life as I took him off. I held him most tenderly in my closed hand, very careful not to crush or even press his tiny perishing body, and breathed into the shut hollow of my palm upon him with a warm and loving breath. I was so very busy, there were so many things to be done that morning, I could not stop to sit down and nurse him back to life. But I held him safe, and as I went up and down the garden paths gathering the rest of my flowers, I breathed every moment into my hand upon him. Ten, fifteen, twenty minutes passed; he made no sign of life. Alas, I thought, he is truly dead; when all at once I felt the least little thrill pass through the still, cold form, an answering thrill of joy ran through me in response, and more softly, closely, tenderly yet I sent my warm breath to the tiny creature as I still went on with my work. In a few minutes more I began to feel the smallest fluttering pulse of life throbbing faintly within him; in yet a few moments more he stirred and stretched his wings, comforting himself in the genial heat. When at last I felt him all alive, I took a small shallow basket of yellow straw, very small and light, and in it put a tuft of soft cotton wool, filled a tiny glass cup with sugar and water, honey-thick, placed it in the basket by the cotton, then gently laid the wee bird on the warm fluff. His eyes were still closed, but he moved his head slowly from side to side. The sun had risen and was pouring floods of light and heat into the garden. I carried the basket out into the corner where the heavenly blue Larkspurs stood behind the snow-whiteness of the full

blossoming Lilies, and among the azure spikes I
hung the pretty cradle where the sunbeams lay
hottest and brightest on the flowers. The wind,
grown balmy and mild, rocked the tall flower-
spikes gently, the basket swayed with them, and
the heat was so reviving that the dear little creature presently opened his eyes and quietly looked
about him. At that my heart rejoiced. It was
delightful to watch his slow return to his old self
as I still went on with my work, looking continually toward him to see how he was getting on.
The ardent sunbeams sent fresh life through him;
suddenly he rose, an emerald spark, into the air,
and quivered among the blue flowers, diving deep
into each winged blossom for his breakfast of
honey.

All day and every day he haunts the garden,
and when tired rests contentedly on the small twig
of a dry pea-stick near the Larkspurs. The rosy
Peas blossom about him, the Hollyhock flowers
unfold in glowing pink with lace-like edges of
white; the bees hum there all day in and out of
the many flowers; the butterflies hover and waver
and wheel. When one comes too near him, up
starts my beauty and chases him away on burnished wings, away beyond the garden's bounds,
and returns to occupy his perch in triumph,—the
dry twig he has taken for his home the whole
sweet summer long. Other humming-birds haunt
the place, but he belongs there; they go and come,
but he keeps to his perch and his Larkspurs faithfully. He is so tame he never stirs from his twig
for anybody, no matter how near a person may

come ; he alights on my arms and hands and hair unafraid; he rifles the flowers I hold, when I am gathering them, and I sometimes think he is the very most charming thing in the garden. The jealous bees and the butterflies follow the flowers I carry also, sometimes all the way into the house. The other day, as I sat in the piazza which the vines shade with their broad green leaves and sweet white flowers climbing up to the eaves and over the roof, I saw the humming-birds hovering over the whole expanse of green, to and fro, and discovered that they were picking off and devouring the large transparent aphides scattered, I am happy to say but sparingly, over its surface, every little gnat and midge they snapped up with avidity. I had fancied they lived on honey, but they appeared to like the insects quite as well.

In the sweet silence before sunrise, standing in the garden I watch the large round shield of the full moon slowly fading in the west from copper to brass and then to whitest silver, throwing across a sea of glass its long, still reflection, while the deep, pure sky takes on a rosy warmth of color from the approaching sun. Soon an insufferable glory burns on the edge of the eastern horizon ; up rolls the great round red orb and sets the dew twinkling and sparkling in a thousand rainbows, sending its first rejoicing rays over the wide face of the world. When in these fresh mornings I go into my garden before any one is awake, I go for the time being into perfect happiness. In this hour divinely fresh and still, the fair face of every flower salutes me with a silent joy that fills me

Home of the Humming-bird

The west gate in the reconstructed garden. John M. Kingsbury photo.

with infinite content; each gives me its color, its grace, its perfume, and enriches me with the consummation of its beauty. All the cares, perplexities, and griefs of existence, all the burdens of life slip from my shoulders and leave me with the heart of a little child that asks nothing beyond its present moment of innocent bliss. These myriad beaming faces turned to mine seem to look at me with blessing eyes. I feel the personality of each flower, and I find myself greeting them as if they were human. "Good-morning, beloved friends! Are all things well with you? And are you tranquil and bright? and are you happy and beautiful?" They stand in their peace and purity and lift themselves to my adoring gaze as if they knew my worship, — so calm, so sweet, so delicately radiant, I lose myself in the tranquillity of their happiness. They seem like sentient beings, as if they knew me and loved me, not indeed as I love them, but with almost a reliance on my sympathy and care, and a pleasure in my delight in them. I please myself with the thought that if anything goes wrong with them, if a vine or tender stalk droops for lack of support, or if some insect is working them woe, or threat of harm comes to them from any quarter, they say to each other, "Patience! She will be coming soon, she will see our trouble, she will succor us, and all will again be well."

The summer life in the garden of the winged things of the air is most charming, — the wonderful creatures that have escaped, as it were, from the earth. The life that crawls and creeps and devours and destroys, in the forms of slug and cutworm and all hideous shapes, is utterly forgotten as we watch these ethereal beings, fluttering, quivering, darting, dancing, wavering, wheeling, rejoicing aloft in merry flight.   The Larkspur spikes bend with the weight of the booming bees, the whole blossoming space is alive with many-colored butterflies like floating flowers, and the humming-birds are a perpetual pleasure.   They are astir even before sunrise, when the air is yet chill with the breath of the retreating night, — there they are, vibrating with their soft humming over the Larkspur blossoms which are themselves like exquisite azure birds all poised for flight, or diving deep into the fragrant trumpets of the Honeysuckle, everywhere flashing in emerald and ruby as the sun's first beams strike them, like the living jewels they are.   Their fearlessness is something amazing.   I never shall forget the surprise of joy that filled me when for the first time one alighted on my sleeve and rested, as much at home as if I were a stick or a harmless twig!   Sparrows and nuthatches had often alighted on my head as I stood musing over my flowers, perfectly still, but to have this tiny spark of brilliant life come to anchor, as it were, on anything so earthly as my arm was indeed a nine days' wonder!   Now it has grown to be an old story, but it is never any less delightful.

August 18th. This morning the garden was so dry again when I sought it at sunrise, in spite of the heavy dew, that I took the hose and turned on the water, showering the whole place most thoroughly. When I had done the drops clung thickly to everything, to the sprays of Sweet Peas especially, the rough surface of their leaves and stalks catching and holding the water more tenaciously than the smoother foliage; they were begemmed, as it were, with so many sparkling spheres of light. The tamest, dearest humming-bird, whose home is in the Larkspurs, was greatly excited by this unexpected and refreshing shower, and whirred about me, uttering continually his one fine, sweet, keen note. When my rain-storm ceased he flew to the Sweet Peas close to his azure bower, and sitting on a green spray already bent with the weight of the clear drops, proceeded to take his morning bath with the most cheerful enjoyment. He fluttered his tiny wings and ducked his head and wagged his tail and drenched himself completely; his feathers were so soaking wet that his little body looked no bigger than a bumble-bee; then he flew up and lighted on the tallest pea-stick that reached over the fence among the Larkspurs: there sitting on his favorite twig he rapidly preened his feathers, shook himself, spread his wings and tail and combed them with his slender beak and dried them in the broad, bright beams that poured across the garden from the low sun. With claws and beak he smoothed and arranged his dainty raiment, perfectly regardless of me, his ardent admirer, standing near enough to touch him with my finger. Then he fluttered in and out among the flowers, dipping into every dewy chalice and feasting on his fragrant honey.

I wonder, as I muse over the charms of these most minute of feathered creatures, how it is possible for their tiny wings to bear them over the miles of restless and perilous brine, to find this rock with its nest of flowers! Do they surmise the hospitality that awaits them at the end of their long journey as they steer their dangerous way across the wastes of the salt sea on those small, weak, quivering pinions? Have they some subtle inkling of the tender welcome that awaits them here? Do they guess how they will be admired and adored? I have filled a small glass mug with sugar and water thick as honey, and fastened it in a crotch of the pea-sticks for them to feed upon; the bees throng to it, the ants have found it, and I hope the humming-birds will feast there too. One morning lately, as I was busy in the garden, a little creature brushed by me so close I thought it was a bee; turning to look at it, I was sure it was a humming-bird, but such an atom! Its like I had never imagined. I watched it, fascinated, as it flew here, there, and everywhere, whirring just like a humming-bird, crazy over the annual Larkspurs. A greenish golden sheen was reflected from the head and back, the very color of the little bird, and it had a small, short tail, with a band of white round its body, which seemed feathered, as also its mottled breast. Its bright black eyes were like the bird's, and it hummed with its wings in precisely the same way. Its beak was short, and as it went from flower to flower, probing for honey, I was perfectly sure it was a new variety of humming-bird, the most minute that was ever created. I watched it with breathless interest, completely puzzled by it. Perfectly tame, it flew all about me and investigated the flowers in my hand. Suddenly I discovered that it had three pairs of legs! No bird, I said, ever had more than one, and then I was satisfied that it must be the most marvelous moth in the world. It was so happy and beautiful, flying about so confidingly in the bright sunshine within reach of my hand! But I knew of some one to whom it would be a treasure, so I threw a light veil over, caught it, and sent it softly to sleep forever with some chloroform. It was *Ællopos Titan*, very rare, and found in the tropics.

The dazzling white Lilies blossoming now, bright as silvery snow below the Larkspurs, are taller than they by several feet. I wish I could in any words paint the hues of these splendid Delphiniums ; such shades of melting blue, some light, others dark, some like the summer heaven, and dashed across their pale azure wings with delicious rose. Now is the garden at high tide of beauty. Sweet Peas are brilliant in all their vivid tints; they are doing bravely, spite of the drought, because their roots are so well shaded. They bloom so plenteously that they can hardly be gathered, though they are cut daily. The Rose Campion bed is a lake of delicate colors with its border of scarlet Flax. Poppies of every tint are blazing; the Hollyhocks are splendid, with their comrades the Sunflowers; every day the single Dahlias surprise me with new and unexpected flowers ; the Tea Rose bed is a perpetual delight and astonishment; the purple Zanzibar Lily is blossoming in its tub and never is without its wonderful cup afloat; the Lotus sends up strong, long-stemmed leaves aloft, and keeps me eagerly looking for its promised flower of radiant pink, — its leaves are a marvel with their mystic markings held so high above the water. The Honeysuckles are breathing out all their sweetness on the air; the Pinks are out in spicy bloom; the Mountain Fringe drapes the doorway with cloudy green and pale rose-color. Constellations of Marigolds and Artemisias and Coreopsis, whole solar systems of fiery suns and stars, blossom all over the place, and in partly shaded corners large fragrant stars of Nicotiana shine also when twilight falls. The Japanese Sunflowers make every spot gay where they unfold; they are hardy; when once they fairly get a foothold in the garden, they will not be dislodged, and I for one would never wish to dislodge them, though they spread and grow and multiply rapidly, and take much space if left to go on undisturbed. They have an indescribable golden atmosphere about them, because, I suppose, of their cup-like shape; they never stretch their petals out flat like other Sunflowers. They have a small brown central disk, and their "ray-like florets" are of deep yellow, curved more inward than outward. The Artemisias are in one shade of full, rich gold, in shape like a common field Daisy; the Marigolds are in every shade of yellow, orange, and flame, effulgent, — some with centres of velvet brown, some with peacock green, some all gold, with exquisite gradations of color

through all their rays. "Ardent Marigolds!"
sang John Keats. Ardent indeed they are, with
fervors of color that glow like the beams of day.

The dark crimson Jacqueminot Roses are almost gone, but almost every other flower is at its
best, the whole garden in blossom at once. Dearly
I love to sit in the sun upon the doorstep with
a blossom in my hand and meditate upon its
details, the lavish elaboration of its loveliness, to
study every peculiar characteristic of each, and
wonder and rejoice in its miraculous existence, a
feast more delicate and satisfying than the honey
the birds and bees and butterflies gather from its
heart. Over my head the Cobœa vine droops its
large green and purple bells, with many another
flower beside. The Tropæolum Lucifer throng-
ing up the trellis on either hand truly merits the
name of Light-bearer; its scarlet velvet blooms
have almost an illuminating quality. I hold a
flower of the pretty Love-in-a-mist, the quaint
Nigella, and scan its charming face. It blossoms
late and long, and is a flower of most distinguished beauty. It is star-shaped, in tints of
white, blue, and purple, with full rich stamens
and anthers of warmer red-purple, the petals on
the back delicately veined in each variety with
fine lines of faint green. The rich cluster of
stamens is surrounded at the base by eight smaller
inner petals in different tints, so wonderful in detail, so ornate in decoration as to be simply indescribable. Each large outer petal is curved and
cup-shaped, yet each has its finishing point which
makes the blossom starry, and these eight inner

petals radiate from the centre within, above the larger ones. The foliage whence it gets its old-time name, Love-in-a-mist, is like a soft green vapor, and in the double varieties, the white especially, runs up and mixes itself with the petals. The single varieties are much the finest. They have a faint perfume of anise, and they are among the quaintest and most interesting flowers I know.

I love to pore over every blossom that unfolds in the garden, no matter what it may be, to study it and learn it by heart as far as a poor mortal may. If one but gazes closely into a tiny flower of the pale blue Forget-me-not, what a chapter of loveliness is there! One sees at a glance the sweet color of the starry, compact cluster, and perhaps will notice that the delicate buds in their cherishing calyx are several shades of rose and lilac before they unclose, but unless one studies it closely, how shall one know that in most cases the *himmel-blau* petals are distinctly heart-shaped, that round its golden centre it wears a necklace of pearls, or so they seem, till on looking closer one discovers that the effect is made by the fluting of the whitened folds of each petal at the base; it looks precisely as if it wore a string of polished beads. The tiny spot of darkness within its inmost yellow ring holds five stamens, with dusty anthers of paler yellow (also heart-shaped when the flower first unfolds) in a close circle round the pistil of pale green. Unless the eyes are young and keen a microscope only will tell this; but it is one of the wisest things in the world to carry in one's pocket a little magnifying

glass, for this opens so many unknown gates into
the wonders and splendors of Creation. There
is such wealth of ornament, such marvelous sub-
tile thought spent on the smallest blossom ! The
" sweet and cunning hand of Nature" is so lavish
of its work, and it is all so happy, the joy is so
inexhaustible, the refreshment to the human soul
so heavenly !

The fragrant fringes of the Mignonette, how
surprising and curiously beautiful they are under
the little pocket microscope! What elaboration
of detail, what tempered harmonies of color, what
marvels of construction ! I reach my hand for a
blossom of Coreopsis Coronata some one has let
fall on the step, — what a refulgent flower! There
is something Spanish about its aspect always to
me. There are eight yellow velvet petals deeply
toothed at the edges, and rich embroideries in
red about the warmer yellow of the centre. Gorgeous it is, and so is its relative, Coreopsis Drummondii, and both have a double row of sepals, the
row nearest the corolla brown and thin and light,
the outer one much coarser and bright green.
The centre of the Drummondii is more like the
wild Rudbeckia, with markings not so ornate as
the Coronata, but in a mass, and of a brighter,
clearer red. All this family of flowers, Lanceolata, Golden Banner, the deep scarlet and maroon
varieties, are superb and most decorative.

It is a great temptation to linger over the loveliness of every flower that unfolds, but I spare
my patient readers, and leave them to pursue
these fascinating researches for themselves.

I have had reward enough for all my care of
the Water Lilies (even though they had put forth
only leaves, but they have blossomed well) in the
delight of the birds over the tubs of clear water
on which the mottled leaves are floating. So
many charming creatures pause at them to drink,
and the song-sparrows bathe there daily. Enchanting it is to watch their pretty ways as they
hop from the tub's edge upon a Lily-pad which
yields beneath their weight and lets them gently
down, but out of this they always flit and take
their own way about it, dipping and splashing
bravely till they are thoroughly drenched, then
preening and drying themselves as they sit upon
the brim, and singing their song of sweet content
when all is done.

September 23d. Now are the crickets loud in
the grass and the Hawkweed waves in pale yellow
all over the island, the autumn Dandelion, starry
on its long and slender stem. But still the garden glows, and still autumn

> "Sets budding more
> And still more later flowers for the bees,
> Until they think warm days will never cease,
> For summer has o'er brimmed their clammy cells."

Where the Hollyhocks earliest to blossom stand
bereft of all save their thick-growing, full, round
seed vessels, the late Morning-glories have
wreathed and twined themselves and hung the
stems with white and rose and heaven-blue bells,
and the later blooming stalks are rich with fresh
flowers. Still the Sweet Peas blossom as if their

thick ranks were ready to fly away with myriad
wings of delicious pink, blue, purple, red, and
white. Poppies yet bloom, Rose Campions at
their brightest, hemmed in with the Scarlet Flax,
and the stars and suns of Marigolds blaze with a
matchless glory. Single Dahlias are sumptuous
in every color, and in their prime. One Coreopsis
Golden Banner is a sight to see, like a great gold
mountain heaped in the middle of the garden.
Many kinds of Helianthus make splendid the little inclosure; Love-in-a-mist puts out flower after
flower of mystic charm; the Asters bloom in
profusion of exquisite colors,—the Comet variety,
which I think is most lovely of all. The white
Stocks are dazzling in their purity, and so fragrant! Nasturtiums run riot, of course, and light
up every corner; the Phloxes glow; the Mourning Brides are fine in their sumptuous black-red
velvet; Verbenas are brilliant; Tea Roses blossoming yet; the Giant Spider flower, *Cloeme
pungens*, rises all over the garden in rosy purple
clouds. Mignonette is lavish of rich spikes of
bloom, and the Pansies never so splendid; immense smooth, perfect flowers of every color, they
never put forth such in the summer heats. Picotee pinks are bright and sweet, but the poor little
Margarets suffered too much with the venomous
carnation worm, spite of my daily care, and are
only just now sending up their buds. I shall take
them up and keep them safe in the house over
the winter. In a corner the deep blue Plum-
bago Lady Larpent blooms finely, the Foxgloves
are strong and tall, though they will not blossom

till another year; but the whole garden is a mass
of bloom and fragance, still haunted by birds,
bees, butterflies, and dragonflies; the humming-
birds are gone, I know not whither, not to return
this year. The withering vines are alive with
many little creepers and warblers and flycatchers;
indeed, the island is full of distinguished bird-
strangers on their way south. Scores of golden
woodpeckers, or flickers, or yellow-hammers (they
have dozens of striking names) are here, and just
now two great ospreys perch on the vane above
the highest ridge-pole, and soar and perch again,
uttering strange, harsh cries. This morning a
large flock of wild geese flew over toward the
south, so low we could see the colors and the
markings of their plumage. The familiar curlews
call sweetly as in spring. Outside the garden
this tranquil morning the soft green turf that
slopes smoothly to the sea in front is shaggy with
the thick dew from which the yet low sun strikes
a thousand broken rainbows. The clumps of
wild Roses glow with their red haws in the full
light; the Elder bushes are laden with clusters of
purple berries; Goldenrod and wild Asters bloom,
and a touch of fire begins to light up the Huckle-
berry bushes, "Autumn laying here and there a
fiery finger on the leaves." The gray rocks show
so fair in the changing lights, and all the dear
island with its sights and sounds is set in the
pale light summer-blue of a smiling sea as if it
were June, with hardly a wave to break its happy
calm. Round the horizon a band of haze, the
same ashes-of-roses color as that which makes

Sunset and the Pinafore

lovely the skies of May, holds the fair world in a
light embrace for this one day; a few white clouds
are losing themselves in the pure blue above; a
few sails gleam afar. Though the tide is full, it
makes no murmur; I hear only the drowsy bees
in the Hollyhocks, the young fledgling song-
sparrows trying their voices, learning the sweet
song their parents are pouring at intervals on the
quiet air, and the chirp and twitter of other birds,
birds of passage, with finch and thrush, nuthatch
and late robin, the whistle of a whitethroat, the
clanking jar of the kingfisher that perches on the
mast of the faithful little tug Pinafore (so many
years our only link with the mainland in winter),
as she lies at her wharf in the upper cove, and
shows his handsome blue and gray plumage and
white collar glittering in the sun. A fisherman
draws his nets in a shining white skiff, but he
makes no sound that I can hear. The season is
so divinely tranquil and sweet, all things are so
beautiful in and about the little isle, from the glittering seal that emerges from the waves to sun
himself sometimes on the seaweed-covered rocks,
to the smallest flower that blossoms in my garden; from the wonderful jelly-fish that spreads its
large diaphanous cup, expanding and contracting
as it swims, and colored like a great melting opal
in the pale-green, translucent water, to the bright-
eyed bats that flitter at dusk when the evening
star is sparkling above the rich red of the sunset
sky. And that reminds me that all summer a
white bat has skittered ghostly with its dark companions, as soon as twilight fell, about the place.

Of a white bat never before have I heard, but all kinds of strange and remarkable creatures find their way here, and I am surprised at nothing.

Once more the weird laughter of the loons comes to my ear, the distance lends it a musical, melancholy sound. From a dangerous ledge off the lighthouse island floats in on the still air the gentle tolling of a warning bell as it swings on its rocking buoy ; it might be tolling for the passing of summer and sweet weather with that persistent, pensive chime.

And so the ripe year wanes. From turfy slopes afar the breeze brings delicious, pungent, spicy odors from the wild Everlasting flowers, and the mushrooms are pearly in the grass. I gather the seed-pods in the garden beds, sharing their bounty with the birds I love so well, for there are enough and to spare for us all. Soon will set in the fitful weather, with fierce gales and sullen skies and frosty air, and it will be time to tuck up safely my Roses and Lilies and the rest for their long winter sleep beneath the snow, where I never forget them, but ever dream of their wakening in happy summers yet to be.

130

*Listed in digram opposite page 73
+Illustrated